TRANSFORMED

TRANSFORMED

How God Renews Your Mind to Make You More Like Jesus

Esther Engelsma

Reformation Heritage Books
Grand Rapids, Michigan

Reformation Heritage Books
3070 29th St. SE
Grand Rapids, MI 49512
616-977-0889
orders@heritagebooks.org
www.heritagebooks.org

Printed in the United States of America
21 22 23 24 25 26/10 9 8 7 6 5 4 3 2 1

Library of Congress Cataloging-in-Publication Data

Names: Engelsma, Esther, author.
Title: Transformed : how God renews your mind to make you more like Jesus / Esther Engelsma.
Description: Grand Rapids, Michigan : Reformation Heritage Books, [2021] | Includes bibliographical references.
Identifiers: LCCN 2021020513 (print) | LCCN 2021020514 (ebook) | ISBN 9781601788894 (paperback) | ISBN 9781601788900 (epub)
Subjects: LCSH: Thought and thinking—Religious aspects—Christianity. | Brain—Religious aspects—Christianity.
Classification: LCC BV4598.4 .E54 2021 (print) | LCC BV4598.4 (ebook) | DDC 230—dc23
LC record available at https://lccn.loc.gov/2021020513
LC ebook record available at https://lccn.loc.gov/2021020514

For additional Reformed literature, request a free book list from Reformation Heritage Books at the above regular or email address.

TO JAMES

*It's an honor to walk life's pathway
with you.*

CONTENTS

PREFACE

Several years ago, the topic of renewing the mind grabbed my attention and began consuming my thoughts. I realized that I knew *what* the Bible instructed me to do with my mind: think on these things, set your mind on things above, bring every thought into captivity, and more. But I wasn't quite sure *how* to follow these instructions in a practical way. They felt lofty and unattainable to a normal Christian like me. How was I supposed to follow them in my everyday life? If I were following them, how would my thought life look different over the next day or hour or minute? If my thought life were different, what impact would that have on my words and actions, my feelings and desires?

At the same time I started asking these questions, I was beginning to feel the impact of the various forms of media I was looking at and listening to. What I was watching, hearing, reading, and seeing was changing me, and I wasn't sure that was a good thing. It seemed that my mind was not being renewed by the word of God but conformed to the world through my media consumption. I was becoming less like Jesus, not more like Him. And I didn't know enough about the process of being transformed by the renewing of my mind to know what needed to be changed in my life.

Over the past few years, I have learned about the renewing of the mind by studying the Bible, books, and the lives of godly people around me. God has used what I have learned to change me. I am not the same person I was before learning about this topic. Though those of us who belong to our faithful Savior Jesus Christ will not be fully transformed until we see Jesus in heaven, God does renew our minds through the knowledge found in the Bible, and He transforms our lives by the renewing of our minds. This book is a record of what I have learned. In six chapters, we will discuss what our minds are and how they are renewed; how our media consumption impacts our thought lives; what it looks like to follow the instructions God gives us about our thought lives; how our thoughts transform what we say and do; what influences our feelings and desires; and how this all culminates in God conforming us to the image of His Son, Jesus Christ.

Though its title is *Transformed*, this book will not transform you. But I hope that it will help you to better understand how God can renew your mind and transform your life, and I hope that this knowledge inspires you to seek Him more. After all, He promises that when you seek, you will find. And so my prayer for this book is simple: that it would motivate you to spend more time in the Book that *does* have transforming power and that it would point you to the One who *can* transform you by the renewing of your mind.

This book would not exist without the help and encouragement of many people. Thank you to my husband, James, for making the time for me to get away with a cup of coffee and a laptop so that I could focus, think, and write; to my kids for letting Mama go write and for asking, "How did your writing go?"; to my dad for the inspiration to write diligently and the willingness to give advice; to my mom for encouraging me and relating to me through writing a book at the same time; to my friends who believed I could finish this book when I wasn't so sure and who encouraged me to keep plodding even when progress was slow. Above all, I give thanks to God—Renewer of minds and Transformer of lives—for the work He does in minds and hearts and the word that He uses to do it.

—1—

THE MIND

Running barefoot down a dirt path with the smell of campfires lingering in the air, anticipating the taste of toasted marshmallows.

Sitting in a creaky chair with a number two pencil in hand and a blank page of circles in front of you, sneaking a look around to see if your classmates are as nervous as you.

Spotting that lone ray of sun piercing through ominous clouds on a dreary day, reminding you of heaven and hope.

Reading words like these changes something in us. Maybe we long for the carefree days of childhood or breathe a sigh of relief that our days of standardized testing are over or glance out the window to see if the sun has come out again.

These reactions happen because God created us with powerful minds. We cannot help but respond to the words and images we take in. In an instant our brains turn these little black marks on a page into thoughts—thoughts that become the words we speak, the actions we take, and the feelings and desires we may or may not want. The thoughts we allow into our minds and the way we respond to them will determine how we live. If we are children of God and desire to give Him glory through a life of obedience and Christlikeness, we must learn to think in obedient, Christlike ways. A merely outward show of righteousness is not what God desires from us; He wants to make us new from the inside out, and that includes the mind.

What Is the Mind?

When most people today think of the mind, they automatically think of the brain, the physical location where thought takes place. But the mind is more than the brain. Rob Moll describes the difference:

> The brain is the physical material that scientists can observe. It is the collection of neurons firing back and forth, the chemicals that lubricate those cellular interactions, and the blood flowing to keep it all working. In contrast, the mind is what can't be seen on an MRI or through any other tool of science. The mind is the collection of thoughts and feelings carried by those cells and chemicals. It is our sense of meaning and purpose, our desires and rationalizations. The brain is like the apparatus upon which the mind works.[1]

Before the days of MRIs and modern scientific tools, the people of the Bible would not have associated the mind with the brain. They would have associated it with the heart because for them, the heart referred to the whole of the inner person—including the mind, the will, and the emotions.[2] This means that the heart was where every thought, every choice, and every feeling came from.[3] A. Craig Troxel writes, "The mind, the desires, and the will are distinct functions of the heart, but they are not separate or unrelated. They constantly influence and relate to one another. This is the way the heart was meant to operate—with knowledge, affection, and volition working with each other."[4]

1. Rob Moll, *What Your Body Knows about God: How We Are Designed to Connect, Serve and Thrive* (Downers Grove, IL: InterVarsity Press, 2014), 22.

2. *Strong's Concordance*, s.v., "*lēbāb*," accessed March 17, 2021, https://www.blueletterbible.org/lang/lexicon/lexicon.cfm?strongs=H3824; and Philip H. Towner, "Mind/Reason," in *Baker's Evangelical Dictionary of Biblical Theology*, ed. Walter A. Elwell (Grand Rapids: Baker Books, 1996), accessed May 8, 2020, https://www.biblestudytools.com/dictionaries/bakers-evangelical-dictionary/mind-reason.html.

3. Michael Barrett, "Conversion: Command and Response" (sermon, Heritage Reformed Congregation, Grand Rapids, Mich., December 2, 2018), https://www.sermonaudio.com/sermoninfo.asp?SID=121181655476621.

4. A. Craig Troxel, *With All Your Heart: Orienting Your Mind, Desires, and Will Toward Christ* (Wheaton, Ill.: Crossway, 2020), 47.

This sounds strange to us because when we hear the word *heart*, we tend to think of how we feel, not how we think. For example, when we say something like "follow your heart," we are talking about acting in a way that is based on feelings. So when we read about the heart in the Bible, we must be careful not to let our cultural context influence us too much. We must remember that when it comes to the heart, thinking and choosing are just as much a part of the heart as feeling. Troxel adds, "It may surprise you that out of all the times that the Hebrew word for 'heart' appears in the Old Testament, our intellectual and rational functions are most often in view. What modern people would attribute to the head or to the brain, Scripture applies to the heart."[5]

To say that someone has a new heart means that because God has worked in her, she is thinking, choosing, and feeling in a new way— one that is more aligned with how God thinks, chooses, and feels. The *Holman Illustrated Bible Dictionary* further explains the connection between the heart and mind: "The heart is connected with thinking: As a person 'thinketh in his heart, so is he' (Prov. 23:7). To ponder something in one's heart means to consider it carefully (Luke 1:66; 2:19). 'To set one's heart on' is the literal Hebrew that means to give attention to something, to worry about it (1 Sam. 9:20). To call to heart (mind) something means to remember something (Isa. 46:8). All of these are functions of the mind, but are connected with the heart in biblical language."[6]

So as we discuss the mind, we must remember that it is a part of the heart as the Bible understands it. Remember the close connection between the mind, the will, and the emotions. While we can speak and think of them separately, they are so interconnected that if there is a change in one, there must necessarily be a change in the others.

---

5. Troxel, *With All Your Heart*, 26.
6. *Holman Illustrated Bible Dictionary* (Nashville: B&H, 2015), 719–20.

What Is a Renewed Mind?

When I sit on the floor with my kids on my lap and open the book *Madeline*, the first words we read are, "In an old house..." Without even needing to look at the page, I recall the next words, "in Paris that was covered in vines."[7] In fact, I don't need to open the book to bring those words to mind. Even as I sit here and type "in an old house" I can't help but fill in the rest of the sentence. Before I was a mom, an old house might have made me think of estate sales and classic wood floors, but it would not have triggered thoughts of Paris and vines. This is because at that point, I had not read *Madeline* many times.

We all experience this in different ways. A song or a smell or a line of poetry triggers a specific memory or piece of information. At a different stage in life, the same song or smell or line would have triggered something different or nothing at all. The input is the same, but because of a change in how our minds think, the output is different. You might say that our minds have been renewed.

But these are only minuscule examples of mind renewal. When the Bible talks about the renewing of our minds, it means something far more grand and glorious than recalling a line of a children's book. Renewing of the mind is the work of the Holy Spirit to renovate, or completely change for the better,[8] the mind of the true Christian. This renewing of the mind is part of sanctification, which the Westminster Shorter Catechism defines in question 35 as "the work of God's free grace, whereby we are renewed in the whole man after the image of God, and are enabled more and more to die unto sin, and live unto righteousness." If we are true Christians, we are in the process of being sanctified, so our minds should begin to think different and more holy thoughts than they did before we were saved. Simply put, we have a new way of thinking.

---

7. Ludwig Bemelmans, *Madeline* (New York: Penguin, 1998), 1.
8. *Strong's Concordance*, s.v., "*anakaínōsis*," accessed February 2, 2021, https://www.blueletterbible.org/lang/lexicon/lexicon.cfm?Strongs=G342&t=NKJV.

Before God saves and starts His renewing work, He is in none of the unbeliever's thoughts (Ps. 10:4). When there are no thoughts of God—no glorifying Him, thanking Him, or knowing Him—then all thoughts are futile, the heart is darkened, and God gives over to a debased mind and to a way of life that is not according to His word (Rom. 1:21, 28). This was often the case for the Israelites (Ps. 81:11–12), and it is the case for many people today. Unbelievers are increasingly conformed to this world (Rom. 12:2) because they are not thinking of God and He is not renewing their minds.

But (praise God!) He does work in the minds and lives of believers, and a key difference is in our thoughts. According to David Saxton, "Psalm 1 clearly distinguishes between the path of those who are wicked and godly. The key dividing line is one's thinking, reasoning, and meditation. This is because these inevitably dictate one's behavior."[9] When unrighteous people forsake their own thoughts and ways and seek God instead, He promises that He will have mercy and abundantly pardon (Isa. 55:6–7).

What does this change of thinking look like in practical daily life? Every day, we are faced with input in the form of information and circumstances. As the Spirit renews our minds, how we react to the information and circumstances changes. Our minds react with different, more holy thoughts than before. Because we are thinking in a different way, our lives show a transformed output of words, actions, and feelings. What once may have produced delight (for example, gossip or sexual sin) begins to produce disgust because we are beginning to think more about how much God hates sin and less about the short-lived pleasure we might receive from the sin. What once sent us into turmoil and seeking distraction (for example, sickness or inconvenience) begins to send us to our heavenly Father in prayer because we are beginning to understand the joy and benefits of prayer and that there are no joy and benefits from other sources of help to which we have turned in the past. What once bored us (for

9. David W. Saxton, *God's Battle Plan for the Mind: The Puritan Practice of Biblical Meditation* (Grand Rapids: Reformation Heritage Books, 2015), 101.

example, the Bible or Christian conversation) begins to enthrall us because we are beginning to place more value on eternal, spiritual life than we place on temporal, physical life. The input is the same but our minds have changed, and so the output—what we say and do and feel in response—has changed.

This does not mean our thought life will be perfectly holy the instant we are saved—perfection will not be ours until heaven (1 John 3:2). It also does not mean our thought life will be automatically and effortlessly holy. As we'll see throughout this book, renewal of the mind happens as we live in obedience to Scripture and the Holy Spirit, which is not always easy. But we can be greatly encouraged that renewal is certain because God promises that He completes the work He begins (Phil. 1:6). He *will* transform us, and He will do it by the renewing of our minds (Rom. 12:2).

Why Does My Mind Need to Be Renewed?

When Adam and Eve were created in the image of God, everything about them, including their minds, was very good. Everything they naturally thought, said, did, felt, and desired aligned with what God thought, said, did, felt, and desired. They were holy, which nineteenth-century minister J. C. Ryle describes as "the habit of being of one mind with God...hating what He hates—loving what He loves—and measuring everything in this world by the standard of His Word."[10] They did not need to struggle against corrupt thoughts or unholy desires because they had been created in His image and were in perfect communion with Him (Gen. 1:27, 31).

But then something happened that broke this perfect alignment. Satan entered the garden in the form of a serpent and spoke words to Eve—words that she *listened* to, that made her begin to think differently than she had thought before. While listening to the serpent, she *spoke* a half-truth about what God's command to her and Adam had been. She began to *think* that God might be lying and that He

---

10. J. C. Ryle, *Holiness: Its Nature, Hindrances, Difficulties, and Roots* (Cambridge: James Clarke, 1956), 34–38.

was keeping something good from her (Gen. 3:1–5). Because she was thinking in this way, she *saw* that the fruit on the tree looked good and delightful, and she began to believe that it might make her wise, like the serpent had said. Everything she heard, said, thought, and saw led to what she *did* next—she took the fruit, ate the fruit, and gave the fruit to Adam (v. 6).

As the serpent had promised, Adam's and Eve's eyes were indeed opened after they ate the fruit, and they did know good and evil, but the knowledge did not make them more like God. It made them less like God. Their eyes had been opened to their nakedness (Gen. 3:7). Their actions had led to *feelings*—of shame, fear, and guilt. They were no longer in communion with God. Their *desire* was to hide from God (vv. 8–13).

Adam and Eve and the whole of the human race had been forever changed by what they had done. There was no way for us to get back to who we were created to be—no way, that is, unless God made a way. "But God, who is rich in mercy, because of His great love with which He loved us" (Eph. 2:4) did make a way. The way turned out to be a person, and His name is Jesus Christ, the Son of God. Jesus was born as a baby in order to grow up and do what Adam had not been able to do—live a life that was perfectly aligned with God in everything He thought, said, did, felt, and desired.

Not only does Jesus provide a perfect example of how we should think and live but He also died on the cross, rose again, and ascended into heaven to provide a way for us to be saved from our sins, renewed in our minds, and transformed in our lives. God promises that to believe on Jesus alone for salvation is to be saved (Acts 16:31), and to be saved is to begin the challenging, beautiful, hopeful journey of sanctification. In sanctification, the Holy Spirit works in our minds and hearts as we grow in knowledge and obedience to make us more like Jesus.

Sanctification is such a hopeful journey because we already know the ending. We know that when we finally see Jesus face-to-face, we will be like Him (1 John 3:2)! We will never again have to struggle against sinful thoughts and their tragic results in our lives.

This hope, this knowledge of how our story ends (or should we say, how our story really begins?), is the evidence of what we can't see yet with our eyes (Heb. 11:1), the motivation to keep on running the race no matter what (12:1), and the energy to love others and to love God above all (Mark 12:30–31). One day, in a state of perfection and glory, we will look back on the light, momentary afflictions we are currently journeying through and be able to say not just with faith but with eyes that see clearly, "God worked all things together for our good [see Rom. 8:28] and His glory [see Isa. 43:7]!"

Who Renews My Mind?

We know now what a renewed mind is and why our minds need to be renewed, but we still need to explore the question of who renews our minds. Is it me, or is it God? How does my responsibility interact with God's sovereignty? Let's try to answer these questions by studying the story of Jericho.

God gave one of the most unusual battle plans in history to Joshua after the Israelites had entered Canaan. The obstacle before them was the walled city of Jericho. God told Joshua, "I have given Jericho into your hand" (Josh. 6:2) and then explained that all the Israelite men of war were to march around the city one time for six days, then seven times on the seventh day. During the final march around the city, the priests were to blow their trumpets, the men of war were to shout, and the city walls were to fall down.

This battle plan was not standard because it was not logical if we think of it in human terms. Merely marching around a city with trumpets and shouts doesn't make its walls fall down, and yet the walls did fall when the Israelites marched. It was clearly God's power that made Jericho tumble to the ground, but it was also God who told the Israelites to march. Could He have conquered Jericho on His own, without the people marching? Yes, He is all-powerful, and there are times when He did conquer without any effort on the part of the Israelites (2 Kings 7:5). But would He have made the walls fall down if the Israelites had not obeyed?

The answer comes in the next chapter. With Joshua's fame spreading through the land of Canaan after the defeat of Jericho, the Israelites thought they would easily win their next battle against Ai, but they were sorely defeated. The reason for their defeat? One man, Achan, had disobeyed God by taking some of the spoil from Jericho. God told Joshua explicitly that because of the sin, the Israelites could not stand before their enemies (Josh. 7:11–12).

Had Israel disobeyed God at Jericho too, it seems that the walls would not have fallen down. The pattern of historical events throughout the Bible shows that God wants our obedience more than He wants a "good outcome." His promises are often if-then statements: if you do this, then that will happen. At the same time, the Bible makes it clear that it is the Holy Spirit who works in our hearts so that we can obey in the first place. Back at Jericho, it wasn't the marching itself that made the walls fall. Yet without trust in God, trust that was given by God, trust that was made evident by the marching, it is likely that God would not have caused the walls to fall. Hebrews 11:30 says, "By faith the walls of Jericho fell down after they were encircled for seven days." God works through the faith and obedience of His people to accomplish the work He wants to do, which involves far more than conquered cities.

This concept is crucial as we consider how God transforms us by the renewing of our minds. We don't renew our minds by ourselves, but God through His Holy Spirit renews us (Titus 3:5) and causes fruit to grow in our lives (Gal. 5:22–23). It is also God who gives specific instructions in the Bible about how we are to think, look, listen, speak, act, feel, and desire. Could He sanctify us on His own, without our obedience? He has the power to do anything. But does He sanctify us if we do not obey? It is not our obedience that causes sanctification, but without trust in God that is made evident by our obedience, God does not work out His sanctification within us. He uses our obedience, worked in us by His Holy Spirit, to accomplish the work He wants to do.

So who is responsible for renewing your mind? Who does the work? Is it you? Yes, in the same way that it was the Israelites who conquered Jericho by walking around it. Is it God? Yes, in the same way that it was God who conquered Jericho by giving the command to walk, providing the power to walk, and making the walls tumble down after the Israelites had walked. God holds all the power, but He still commands us to obey.

How Is My Mind Renewed?

When the Israelites walked around Jericho, they were not doing so as robots, programmed to march around the city. God had given them a command, and they could choose whether they would obey it or not. In this case they chose to obey, and their choice had an effect. The walls of Jericho came tumbling down.

Like the Israelites, we possess the ability to use our minds to make choices, even to choose how we think. God has given us many commands in the Bible, and we can choose to obey by the power of the Spirit. And like the Israelites walking around Jericho, we experience both visible and invisible effects as a result of our choices.

One of these effects is that the physical matter that makes up our brains actually changes over time based on what we learn, think about, experience, and do. Caroline Leaf writes, "As you think, you choose, and as you choose, you cause genetic expression to happen in your brain. This means you make proteins, and these proteins form your thoughts. Thoughts are real, physical things that occupy mental real estate."[11] This is a concept called neuroplasticity, which "by definition means the brain is malleable and adaptable, changing moment by moment of every day. Scientists are finally beginning to see the brain as having renewable characteristics (as in Rom. 12:2)."[12] Rob Moll explains the idea further: "Our brains are always changing based on new experiences and new information. Neurons form new 'arms' called dendrites and axons and connect to one another, making physical changes in the brain that allow us to recall a memory or information. Change doesn't come easily, but as we establish new

---

11. Leaf, *Switch On Your Brain*, 32.
12. Leaf, *Switch On Your Brain*, 22.

patterns of thinking and habits, the neural pathways that were once new and difficult grow firmer and more well traveled."[13]

This is both sobering and encouraging. It is sobering because what we might view as stray thoughts or inconsequential decisions have great impact on our physical brains and therefore on our minds. It is encouraging because it means God created us in a way that allows for the possibility of renewal and sanctification and having the mind of Christ! We don't have to stay stuck in sinful ruts of thinking. As Mark Kelderman observes, "Every day that passes, every time we open the Scriptures, we are not the same person. We have either progressed or regressed. There is no standing still in the spiritual life."[14]

When the Holy Spirit helps us to grow in knowledge of (Col. 3:10) and obedience to (Rom. 6:16) God and His word, we are changed. The way we think is changed, and the physical matter that makes up our brains is changed. And God is the one who designed it this way. God designed us so that everything we think forms us into who we are (Prov. 23:7). It is no coincidence, then, that He gave us commands like "think on these things" (Phil. 4:8 KJV) and "set your mind" (Col. 3:2; see also Rom. 8:5–8), which He works through to change us for the better, to make us think and act more like Christ if we will only obey them. It is no coincidence that in the Bible He gave us knowledge of Himself and the world that is meant to form the way we think so that it aligns more and more with how God thinks (Col. 3:9–10). It is no coincidence that He puts us in circumstances to test how we will react (Deut. 8:2; Jer. 17:9–10)—circumstances that make it evident whether we are really trusting God and loving our neighbor.

If we were robots, God would not use commands, knowledge, and circumstances to work change in our hearts. A robot only needs reprogramming by its creator. But we are not robots. Our loving

---

13. Moll, *What Your Body Knows about God*, 157.
14. Mark Kelderman, "Grow in Grace" (sermon, Heritage Reformed Congregation, Grand Rapids, Mich., October 28, 2018), https://www.sermonaudio.com/sermoninfo.asp?SID=102718213810.

Creator did not program us but designed us, and we can be sure that the Creator who has designed us so precisely also has a purpose to work together every command, every piece of knowledge, and every circumstance for the good of those who love Him—to conform our way of thinking not to the world but to the mind of Christ (Rom. 8:28–29; Phil. 2:5).

What Changes When My Mind Is Renewed?

To be conformed to the image of Christ, to have His mind in me, sounds wonderful, but what does it really mean? What changes when we start thinking like Christ? What difference does it make to have a mind that is being renewed?

The difference is total transformation (Rom. 12:2). When we begin to think differently, we also begin to look, listen, speak, act, feel, and desire differently. Our thoughts impact every other part of our lives. In order to really grasp this, we need to break down what goes on in our hearts.

Remember that the heart is the whole of the inner person. It includes the mind (how we think), the will (how we choose what to look at, listen to, say, and do), and the emotions (how we feel and what we desire). Each of these components influences the others. A. Craig Troxel emphasizes this: "Our desires and our will significantly influence our mind, just as our thinking affects our desires and will. God shaped our hearts in such a way that our thinking functions properly only if our desires and will are right with God."[15] To better grasp how these components of the heart work together, look at the picture on the next page. To draw the heart this way is to oversimplify it because the components are so intertwined in our inner person that they are really inseparable. Each component should really have an arrow drawn to and from every other component. But seeing it simplified in this way will help us think through what the impact of each component is.

---

15. Troxel, *With All Your Heart*, 57–58.

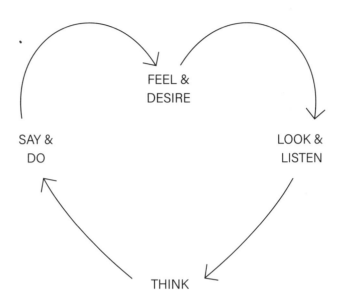

Because of the way the world thinks, it likes to start at the top of this drawing. It tells us that what we feel and desire is "our truth" and that we should base our choices and our thinking on that. When we do, what we "naturally" (that is, sinfully) feel and desire becomes the basis of what we look at and listen to. Our choice of information that we take in through shows, movies, social media, news, books, and music is based on what we feel like watching and hearing. Our thoughts are shaped by all this (often worldly) information that we are taking in, conforming us to the world without us even realizing it. As our thoughts are conformed, we begin to speak and act more and more like the world. This feels good and right to us because it aligns with our "natural" (sinful) feelings and desires, and the cycle continues.

In Scripture, God offers a very different way of life to follow. Sinclair Ferguson explains it this way:

> God made men and women capable of thinking, willing, and feeling. In the divine design, our thinking was meant to be informed, shaped and governed by his revelation. We were

created to think God's thoughts after him, as it is sometimes put. Such thought processes inevitably inform, influence and direct our powers of volition. We understand what is right and good, and we commit our wills to accomplishing it. In turn our feelings are moulded by what we think and will. In a rightly-ordered life, emotions or feelings are directed to what is good and gracious; those things are desired and loved. Our feelings and emotions are not isolated from our thinking and willing but guided by them.[16]

God does not tell us to think and act according to what we naturally feel and desire. Instead, He tells us what we should look at, listen to, think, say, do, feel, and desire, and then He promises that life and joy and peace are the result of following His instructions.

Look: Turn away my eyes from looking at worthless things, and revive me in Your way. (Ps. 119:37)

Listen: Incline your ear, and come to Me. Hear, and your soul shall live. (Isa. 55:3)

Think: You will keep him in perfect peace,
        Whose mind is stayed on You,
        Because he trusts in You. (Isa. 26:3)

Say: He who guards his mouth preserves his life. (Prov. 13:3)

Do: If you know these things, blessed are you if you do them. (John 13:17)

Feel: The fruit of the Spirit is love, joy, peace, longsuffering, kindness, goodness, faithfulness, gentleness, self-control. (Gal. 5:22–23)

Desire: Delight yourself also in the LORD, and He shall give you the desires of your heart. (Ps. 37:4)

16. Sinclair B. Ferguson, *Let's Study Philippians* (Edinburgh: Banner of Truth, 2018), 102.

We function best when we obey God's commands because He created us to live in obedience to Him. When we do obey, we choose to look at and listen to information that helps us grow in the knowledge of God. Because we are growing in the knowledge of God, the way we think is changed, conformed to Christ rather than to the world. Because we are thinking more like Christ, we begin to speak and act more like Him. This feels good and right to us because it is the way we were created to live. It is who we will someday be in perfection (Phil. 1:9–11).

Let's break it down even further by looking at a few specific examples. The table below oversimplifies the concept, but we need to see clearly how our thoughts are a key turning point in everything we choose and feel. While we may not always be able to choose what we see or hear, what we think is always a choice, and it is a choice that has consequences because it determines what we say, do, feel, and desire.

Look/Listen	Think	Say/Do	Feel/Desire
You hear gossip.	*I want to share a piece of gossip I heard.*	You share the gossip.	You feel excited about being in the know. You desire to hear and share more gossip.
	God does not approve of gossip. It betrays others and separates close friends (Prov. 11:13; 16:28).	You walk away from the conversation.	You feel God's pleasure through a clear conscience. You desire to continue to have a clear conscience.

Look/Listen	Think	Say/Do	Feel/Desire
You see someone doing something that annoys you. ↗	*I don't like that. Why do they have to be that way?*	You say something critical.	You feel relieved that you let your feelings out. You desire to continue speaking critically.
↘	*Although I don't like that, I will choose to think about that person's positive traits* (Phil. 4:8).	You say something encouraging.	You feel love and appreciation for the person. You desire to continue building the person up.
You watch a movie with a scene that convicts your conscience. ↗	*This isn't a big deal. It will be over in a minute.*	You continue to watch the movie.	You feel excited because of what you just watched. You desire to watch more.
↘	*This is not pleasing to God. Like Job, I will make a covenant with my eyes* (Job 31:1).	You stop watching the movie.	You feel relieved that you listened to your conscience. You desire more and more to please God.

The simple conclusion is this: if we do not follow God's commands, the result is negative—a cycle that continually plunges us into deeper and greater sin and eventually ends in spiritual death. If we do follow His commands, the result is positive—a cycle that continually grows our holiness and conformity to Christ and eventually brings us to spiritual, eternal life. If we have believed on Jesus alone for salvation, then God is working in us to renew our minds. But we must still walk in obedience to Him by the power of His Spirit. As we do, God uses the renewal that is happening in our minds to bring about the profound transformation in our lives that only He can work, by His grace and for His glory.

2

LOOK AND LISTEN

For much of my life, I did not connect what I ate with how I felt. While I knew that eating too much would cause a stomachache, I did not pay attention to how my body reacted in less extreme situations to healthy or less healthy foods. Then I befriended several women who had allergies to certain types of food. As I learned about how they figured out what they could or could not eat based on how their bodies reacted, I began to pay more attention to what I ate and how my body reacted. As I got into the habit of paying attention, I began to realize which types of meals helped me feel good and energetic and which did not. These realizations changed the way I ate because I was starting to base my food choices on how I would feel later, not on what I was craving at the moment.

As my diet changed, I began to realize that just as what I consumed with my mouth formed and fueled my body, so what I consumed with my eyes and ears was forming and fueling my mind and soul. My body could not digest quality nutrients if I was not eating quality food, and my mind would not think holy thoughts if it was not consuming the proper information. The thoughts my mind was producing were directly connected with everything that I was watching, reading, and listening to. This is how God created us and why He gives commands in the Bible about what (and what not) to look at and listen to. I had to consider the impact of what I was allowing into my mind and question whether it lined up with Scripture or whether I needed to change my diet. Both my body and my mind could only digest what I had chosen to consume. Neither could be renewed unless my choices were healthy and holy.

What You Consume Shapes Who You Are

Whether we are deciding what to consume with our bodies or with our minds, there are countless options to choose from. Everything that we consume by looking with our eyes or listening with our ears—shows, movies, videos, social media, news, books, magazines, and music—is digested with our minds. Whether we realize it or not, and whether we want it to or not, every image, word, phrase, conversation, post, and article has an impact on how we think. The impact may be very tiny, but when added together with a thousand other tiny impacts, it becomes very big. The sum of what we are consuming is used either by Satan to conform us to the world or by God to transform us into the image of Christ by the renewing of our minds. Joel Beeke and Mark Jones write, "The Puritans warned that if ever we would resist the devil's attacks, we must guard what we let into our souls by our ears and eyes."[1] What we look at and listen to is shaping how we think, what we do, and who we are.

Some time ago, I began following several Instagram accounts focused on the topic of minimalism. The ladies who ran these accounts shared pictures and videos of how they had simplified their homes and lives by getting rid of clutter and keeping only the items that they used regularly. After a few weeks of following these accounts, I was surprised to realize that every time I walked into a room in my house, my automatic response was to look around to see if there was anything I could get rid of. That was how quickly my thoughts and mind had been "renewed" by information I was consuming for a mere couple of minutes each day.

This example may seem harmless, but think of the implications. We can't help but be changed by what we take in. That is how God created us, and it is good—as long as what we take in is changing

---

1. Joel R. Beeke and Mark Jones, *A Puritan Theology* (Grand Rapids: Reformation Heritage Books, 2012), 863.

us in a way that makes us more like Him, not more like the world. But so often we don't realize how easily we are influenced, and we are careless about what we consume mentally. The Bible speaks of Lot tormenting his soul by seeing and hearing the lawless deeds of those around him (2 Peter 2:8), and we are often like him. We set our eyes and ears on something without realizing that we are setting our minds—and therefore our hearts—on it.

In his *Confessions*, fourth-century church father Augustine gives an example of a young man named Alypius who was repulsed by the idea of the savage games that took place in the amphitheater in Rome. When his friends dragged him along to one of the games, "he protested that even if they forced his body inside, and held it there, they could not fix his eyes and attention on what was occurring." They did force him inside, and when they sat down, "he shut tight his eyes to seal in his soul against this evil." But his ears were not shut, and what he heard made him curious: "That shout, entering his ears, made his eyes fly open. The mind thus buffeted and overthrown was more rash than steady, and all the weaker for reliance on itself rather than on [God].... *No longer the person he was when he entered*, he was now entered into the crowd, at one with those who forced him there."[2]

We are no less vulnerable than Alypius to being changed by what we see and hear. The difference for us is that we can see and hear almost anything with a mere click of a mouse or tap on a screen. Satan knows this, and he uses it to his advantage. He makes it so easy for us to click and tap without thinking, following every link and whim without realizing how we are being shaped. He does everything he can to make the words and images that will lead to the death of our souls more appealing and exciting than the Word of life. He knows that even if he doesn't get us to slip up in major ways, simply filling our time with seemingly harmless words and images will keep us from time spent in the Bible, starving us of the nutrients we need to grow up in our spiritual lives. In order to fight against the devil, we

---

2. Augustine, *Confessions*, trans. Garry Wills (New York: Penguin, 2006), 121. Italics added.

must be aware of his tactics. Just as I needed to change the way I ate by focusing more on the impact food would have on my body, so we need to change what we consume with our minds by focusing more on what our consumption is shaping us to be.

Look to Christ

If you are a Christ follower, your desire is to be shaped into the image of Christ. That will only happen if you are looking to Christ by trusting Him alone for salvation, seeking Him through prayer, and listening to His word far more than you are looking at and listening to the world around you. In an age when an endless stream of information is constantly available for you to look at, algorithmically chosen to appeal to you specifically, this can be difficult. Because we are sinners, it may not feel easy or natural at first to turn to Christ and His word more than we turn to other forms of media. It can take deliberate and intense effort to begin to choose reading the Bible over scrolling through social media, listening to a sermon over turning on the radio, or picking up a good book over clicking "next episode." This is not to say we must cut other forms of media out of our lives completely but that we must be very careful about our choices. What do our choices tell us about our priorities? Where are we spending our time? What can we learn by comparing today's screen-time statistics on our phones with the amount of time our Bibles were open in our laps? Are we more influenced by the people we follow online or by the Jesus we claim to be followers of?

When we "follow" someone on social media, we click a button so that we will automatically see what they post. Every time they post, we learn a little bit more about who they are, how they live, or what their perspective is on a certain issue. As we look at their posts and learn from them, our own minds and lives are shaped by them. This is not all bad. We were created to be discipled, but we must be careful that those who are discipling us are heading in a direction that we want to go—not being conformed to the world but being transformed into the image of Jesus.

Jesus Himself is our ultimate example of who to be, how to live, and what perspectives to hold. So how do we look to Him? In an age of following others, how do we follow Him? The first step is simple: we study our Bibles. That is where we discover who He is. That is where we find the stories of how He lived. That is where we hear the words that He spoke and learn the perspectives that He held. If we want to be like Him, that is where we must turn. Michael Barrett writes, "The more we see of Christ, the more we will be like Him.... If Christ is the pattern for sanctification, and being conformed to Christ is the consequence of seeing Him, it is essential that we look where He is. The only place we can find the real Christ is in the Word of God.... Therefore, it is vital for us to be in the Word, daily searching for the Savior. He is our pattern for living."[3]

This is how we can fight the appeal of the world and learn to love Jesus more and more. Seventeenth-century Puritan John Owen states, "To draw our hearts away from the world we must fix our eyes on Jesus."[4] When we see the face of Jesus by learning about who He is in the Scriptures, we are seeing the glory of God, and that transforms us (2 Cor. 3:16–18; 4:6). When we dig into the stories of how He lived His life, we find the strength to run the race of our own lives with endurance (Heb. 12:1–2). The Bible tells us "that when He is revealed, we shall be like Him, for we shall see Him as He is" (1 John 3:2). So why not see as much of Him as possible while we are still on earth? Why not pay less attention to the words of the world and far more attention to the word of God?

Listen to the Word

Every day we consume many different words in many different forms, and the ideas these words plant in our minds have a strong influence over how we think, what we do, and how we feel. We must become more aware of the influence that our consumption has

---

3. Michael Barrett, *Complete in Him: A Guide to Understanding and Enjoying the Gospel* (Grand Rapids: Reformation Heritage Books, 2017), 226.
4. John Owen, *Spiritual-Mindedness* (Edinburgh: Banner of Truth, 2016), 137.

on our minds and souls. J. Alisdair Groves and Winston T. Smith write, "Words are powerful. Words that we read and hear shape our perspectives....They reinforce our perspectives or undercut them, focus our attention or distract us, force us to pause or hurry us along. This is not just a possibility or even a strong likelihood. It is inevitable. The words we are exposed to mold our hearts far more than we think. Which words do you want shaping the way you see and respond to the world?"[5]

Human words are powerful. Just think of how one cutting remark or one encouraging compliment can change the course of someone's entire life. But God's words are vastly more powerful! He created the entire world using just words, and He gave us an entire book filled with His words. It is through God's words that He works faith in our hearts, sanctifies us, and gives life:

> So then faith comes by hearing, and hearing by the word of God. (Rom. 10:17)

> Sanctify them by Your truth. Your word is truth. (John 17:17)

> For the word of God is living and powerful, and sharper than any two-edged sword, piercing even to the division of soul and spirit, and of joints and marrow, and is a discerner of the thoughts and intents of the heart. (Heb. 4:12)

> For this reason we also thank God without ceasing, because when you received the word of God which you heard from us, you welcomed it not as the word of men, but as it is in truth, the word of God, which also effectively works in you who believe. (1 Thess. 2:13)

> So shall My word be that goes forth from My mouth;
> It shall not return to Me void,
> But it shall accomplish what I please,
> And it shall prosper in the thing for which I sent it. (Isa. 55:11)

---

5. J. Alasdair Groves and Winston T. Smith, *Untangling Emotions* (Wheaton, Ill.: Crossway, 2019), 125–26.

But for God to work through His word, we must be in His word. And that starts with the simple motion of putting down our phones and picking up our Bibles. Nineteenth-century preacher C. H. Spurgeon writes,

> The passages of Scripture which prove that the instrument of our sanctification is the Word are very many. The Spirit of God brings to our mind the precepts and doctrines of truth, and applies them with power. These are heard in the ear, and being received in the heart, they work in us to will and to do of God's good pleasure. The truth is the sanctifier, and *if we do not hear or read the truth, we shall not grow in sanctification.* We only progress in sound living as we progress in sound understanding.[6]

Just as God told Israel to do *something*—walk—so that the walls of Jericho would fall, He tells us to do *something*—pray, read, study[7]—so that He will work in our hearts through His word. It is not the mere reading that works faith in our hearts, and God is not limited in His power to work only in those who spend the most time reading their Bibles. But He does tell us that this is His normal way of working in our hearts. Being aware of this can help us choose to spend more time under the influence of Scripture. Abigail Dodds says, "Whenever we read the Bible well, far more is happening than we perceive in the moment, just like when we watch our favorite shows. God's thoughts are entering the human mind—more than we can count, much less isolate—making themselves at home, and introducing themselves to whatever ideas they find. While we may focus on a verse or two while reading a chapter, we are standing under a waterfall of teaching, and absorbing much more than we realize."[8]

6. C. H. Spurgeon, *Morning and Evening: Daily Readings by C. H. Spurgeon* (Ross-shire, Scotland: Christian Focus, 2008), 392. Italics added.

7. For helpful resources on studying the Bible, see Jen Wilkin, *Women of the Word: How to Study the Bible with Both Our Hearts and Our Minds* (Wheaton, Ill.: Crossway, 2014); or "The Abide Method," Bible Study Tools: Tools for Moms, Risen Motherhood.com, https://www.risenmotherhood.com/abide.

8. Abigail Dodds, "We Become What We Watch: What Entertainment Does to

Do we really believe in the power God's word has over our minds? If so, how can we not be willing to trade in some of the time we spend looking at and listening to various forms of media for God's word and other information that will help us to grow in the grace and knowledge of our Lord?

God Must Open Your Eyes and Ears

Before continuing, I must reinforce this crucial truth: it is God who has to open our eyes and ears to see and hear what we need. Yes, God works through the knowledge we consume to renew our minds, but the knowledge has no power in itself. God must work through it. Paul explains this to the Corinthians when he describes the difference between unbelievers and believers:

> Even if our gospel is veiled, it is veiled to those who are perishing, whose minds the god of this age has blinded, who do not believe, lest the light of the gospel of the glory of Christ, who is the image of God, should shine on them. For we do not preach ourselves, but Christ Jesus the Lord, and ourselves your bondservants for Jesus' sake. For it is the God who commanded light to shine out of darkness, who has shone in our hearts to give the light of the knowledge of the glory of God in the face of Jesus Christ. (2 Cor. 4:3–6)

Paul also prays for the Ephesians, that God would give them "the spirit of wisdom and revelation in the knowledge of Him" (Eph. 1:17). We could spend our whole lives reading the Bible, but if God does not work in our hearts, it won't do us any good. Our prayer to Him must be, "Open my eyes, that I may see wondrous things from Your law" (Ps. 119:18).

Our Minds," Articles, Desiring God, October 6, 2019, https://www.desiringgod.org /articles/we-become-what-we-watch.

What You Consume Is Your Choice

Even as we acknowledge (and celebrate) God's sovereignty, we must remember our responsibility. Understanding that it is God who works in us does not mean we wait for a magical feeling before we make changes to what we are looking at and listening to. When our conscience convicts us that a certain media choice is not holy, we do not necessarily give it up because we no longer feel any desire for it. We give it up because we believe God when He says, "There is a way that seems right to a man, but its end is the way of death" (Prov. 14:12). When we feel a conviction from the Holy Spirit to spend more time in prayer or more time in the Bible, we do not necessarily obey because we feel an intense desire to pray or read. We obey because we believe God when He says, "Let your heart retain my words; keep my commands, and live" (Prov. 4:4).

The Bible makes it clear that what we look at and listen to is a choice we must make. We are given many examples of godly people who made decisions to consume (or not consume) in holy ways. Job made a covenant with his eyes not to look with lust at a young woman (Job 31:1) so that his heart would not follow after his eyes (v. 7). David determined that he would focus on God's precepts and ways (Ps. 119:15). He could not have been a man after God's own heart (Acts 13:22) if this had not been his focus. Each choice, each byte of information we consume, will turn our hearts toward the world or toward God. C. S. Lewis describes the effect of this turning:

> Every time you make a choice you are turning the central part of you, the part of you that chooses, into something a little different from what it was before. And taking your life as a whole, with all your innumerable choices, all your life long you are slowly turning this central thing either into a heavenly creature or into a hellish creature: either into a creature that is in harmony with God, and with other creatures, and with itself, or else into one that is in a state of war and hatred with God, and with its fellow creatures, and with itself.[9]

---

9. C. S. Lewis, *Mere Christianity* (New York: Macmillan, 1977), 86–87.

Consume What You Desire to Crave

We can be aware of the impact of our choices but still struggle with craving what is not good for our bodies or minds. This is not a new problem for the human race. The Israelites struggled with it long ago. There is an example in the Old Testament of the terrible thing that happens when God allows people to binge on what they are craving:

> They tested God in their heart
>> by demanding the food they craved....
>
> He caused the east wind to blow in the heavens,
>> and by his power he led out the south wind;
> he rained meat on them like dust,
>> winged birds like the sand of the seas;
> he let them fall in the midst of their camp,
>> all around their dwellings.
> And they ate and were well filled,
>> for he gave them what they craved.
> But before they had satisfied their craving,
>> while the food was still in their mouths,
> the anger of God rose against them,
>> and he killed the strongest of them
>> and laid low the young men of Israel.
>>> (Ps. 78:18, 26–31 ESV)

We are aware that what we consume has a great impact, that it shapes who we are and can lead to a devastating outcome. But so often we still crave what we know is not good for us. How can this change? How can we begin craving what is good for our minds and souls?

We begin by changing what we consume. Instead of consuming what we crave, we consume what we desire to crave. If we eat a lot of junk food, what we will crave is more of the same. If we become aware of the negative effects the junk food is having on our bodies, our craving for the junk food is not instantly gone, but we may feel more motivation to eat healthy food instead of junk. The more we live according to what we know we should eat (instead of according to what we desire to eat), the more we will consume healthy food. This decreases our appetite for junk food in the moment, and over time we begin to genuinely crave healthy food because of how good it makes us feel. When we go back to junk food, we notice more than ever before how bad we feel after consuming it, and this reinforces healthy eating.

Our minds are the same way. We might crave mental "junk food"—an overabundance of social media, a song that is inappropriate, a TV show that triggers sinful thoughts—but when we realize the impact this consumption has on our thoughts, words, actions, feelings, and desires, then we can be more motivated to choose differently. Even when we don't feel like it, we can feed our minds with Scripture before scrolling on our phones, with a Christian audio book instead of a secular radio station in the car, with good books over TV shows. David Saxton writes, "When a person feeds his heart with the unhealthy food of the world, he no longer has an appetite for the hearty spiritual feast enjoyed by meditation."[10] The opposite is also true. Fill up on the good stuff first, and your appetite for the junk will begin to decrease. God works through biblical and godly sources of knowledge to decrease our craving for the mental junk food both in the moment and over time. Our sinful cravings won't disappear completely until heaven, but we can see a difference as we live by the Spirit instead of by our cravings.

I have heard stories about Christians who have a dramatic conversion experience and an instant desire and passion for the Bible, but this is not the case for everyone. For many of us who have repented of our sins and believed savingly in Jesus, the decrease in appetite for worldly media and the increase in desire for godly knowledge happen very slowly. In my own life, I had been a Christian for several years before I became truly consistent in reading and studying the Bible every day. And it took at least a year of daily commitment before I was surprised to realize I truly enjoyed, looked forward to, and craved my time in the Bible. Trevin Wax writes,

> The way the Bible does its work on our hearts is often not through the lightning bolt, but through the gentle and quiet

---

10. Saxton, *God's Battle Plan for the Mind*, 122.

rhythms of daily submission, of opening up our lives before this open Book and asking God to change us. Change doesn't always happen overnight. Growth doesn't happen in an instant. Instead, it happens over time, as we eat and drink and exercise…. This is an ordinary routine, yes, but ordinary routines can change your life.[11]

The effect of routine, Spirit-empowered reading and study is that the word of God feeds our minds, fuels our souls, and becomes a joy. As Jeremiah states, "Your word was to me the joy and rejoicing of my heart" (Jer. 15:16). I can testify that this is true for me, and if it has not been your experience yet, keep feeding on God's word and looking to Christ in faith that God will work the joy and rejoicing of your heart too.

Focus on Future Health

Even when studying the Bible feels more mundane than joyful, we can persevere because of the benefits we know it will bring. Cancer patients go to their chemotherapy or radiation appointments not because they sound fun or enjoyable but because patients believe that treatment has the potential to save their life. They are not mad at their doctor for the agony these appointments put them through. They are thankful to their doctor for helping them fight for their life.

We may not have cancer in our bodies, but we all have cancer in our souls, and that cancer is sin. Because of sin, turning our eyes from looking at worthless things (Ps. 119:37) and instead living in God's ways does not sound fun or enjoyable to most of us. Yet we should not be mad at God for taking away what we think we enjoy. We should be thankful to Him because what He is telling us to do will eventually lead to life instead of death. Giving up worthless things might feel like death because it is. It is the death of the deeds of the body (Rom. 8:13). It is the crucifixion of the passions and desires of

---

11. Trevin Wax, "Routine Bible Reading Can Change Your Life," Sections: Bible and Theology, Lifeway Voices, December 3, 2018, https://lifewayvoices.com/bible-theology/routine-bible-reading-can-change-your-life/.

the flesh (Gal. 5:24). It is death that is required if we want to truly live in and by the Spirit (Rom. 8:13; Gal. 5:25).

This future-focused mentality is crucial if we are going to walk consistently by the Spirit and according to God's word. It is a mentality that requires faith. William Boekestein discusses how to use the shield of faith when Satan shoots darts of temptation at us:

> What faith does is allows us to see around that temptation. Do you know what's on the backside of every temptation? Destruction. And faith allows us to see to the backside. It allows us to see the pain of giving in. Wouldn't that be amazing if we would have eyes to see what would happen if we gave in to our temptations? That's what faith is. Faith is also the ability to see around temptation positively, to say, "If I withstand this temptation, I will experience joy! I will have defeated one of the tricks of the devil, and I will be living more victoriously."[12]

In our world today, we will need to defend against daily, maybe even hourly, darts of temptation that Satan shoots at us to get us to look at and listen to what will conform us more to the world. He laces his darts with bits of truth, telling us that giving in will bring pleasure. It often does, but he conveniently leaves out that the pleasure is only momentary and the long-lasting results of sin are devastating. If we are to resist him, we must focus on the end of the wicked (Ps. 73:17–22).

The focus of the Bible and God's people is the opposite of Satan's focus. The Bible tells us that Christians will suffer and must endure but that the reward of faith and walking in the ways of God is far greater and more glorious than anything we can imagine (2 Cor. 4:17–18). The book of Hebrews gives many examples of people who were future focused. The recipients of the letter of Hebrews were able to joyfully accept the plundering of their property because they knew they had a better and abiding possession (10:34). Abraham was willing to leave Ur without knowing where he was going because he looked forward

---

12. William Boekestein, "Put On Your Armor" (sermon, HRC Youth Camp, Hastings, Mich., July 11, 2019), https://www.sermonaudio.com/sermoninfo.asp?SID=722191921567.

to the city designed and built by God (11:10). Moses was willing to be mistreated with the Israelites rather than enjoy the fleeting pleasures of sin because he was looking to the reward (vv. 24–26). Others were able to endure torture because they knew they would rise again to a better life (v. 35). Jesus was able to endure the cross because of the joy that was set before Him (12:2).

This is what faith does for us. It slowly removes the cancer of sin. It allows us to look past the present and see what the effects of our choices will be. It gives evidence of what we do not see yet—that if we look at Christ and listen to His word, we will be far better off than if we look at and listen to the world.

Fast for a Time

So how does our future-focused faith influence us today? How does it change the choices we make about what to look at and listen to? To find out, let's return to our body-mind analogy. When I first became friends with several women who were allergic to different foods, they explained one method for figuring out what their allergies were. They began by cutting a food or group of foods out of their diet for a certain period. Then they slowly added the foods back in, paying close attention to how they felt after eating. This helped them figure out what foods they should avoid completely and what they should eat only in moderation. Because every person's body is different, there is no standard list of allergies. Each of my friends had to figure out how her body was impacted by different foods.

Because each of us has a different mind and soul, we are not all affected in the same way by different types of media, and the Bible does not give us a standard list of what is right and what is wrong for us to consume. Some forms of media, such as pornography, are clearly sinful. Other forms of media, such as news or social media, are not as clear-cut. Consumed in moderation, they may not have negative effects on the mind, just as consuming desserts in moderation is not harmful to your body. But a diet of mostly desserts would lead to poor bodily health, and a mental diet of mostly news or social media or other forms of media, at the expense of the word of God, leads to poor mental health. What we feed our minds is directly connected to what our thought life, and therefore our whole life, is focused on.

Great wisdom is needed to determine how much we should consume of media forms that are not inherently sinful. For example, people who are prone to worry may need to have a stricter limit on the number of news articles they read than those who do not struggle with worry. People who are easily tempted to set their hearts and hopes on material things may need to unsubscribe from sales emails that would not even affect those who do not struggle with materialism. People who have a history of sexual sin may need to cut out any and all forms of media that are even remotely suggestive, even though others may not understand why they feel the need to be so strict. It is important to examine your heart and be honest about where you are likely to be tempted, and then to "lay aside every weight, and the sin which so easily ensnares us" (Heb. 12:1). John Owen writes, "Consider what ways, what kinds of company, what opportunities, what studies, what occupations, what conditions have at any time given, or do usually give, advantages to your sins, and set yourself against them all. Men will do this with their bodily infirmities. The season, the diet and the air that have proved offensive are avoided. Are the things of the soul of less importance?"[13]

How can we know what we can consume in moderation and what we should avoid completely? We can practice the same method as those who are trying to figure out which foods they are allergic to. If you think a specific media (for example, a TV show, a genre of books, or a type of social media account) might be tying you to the world or making you more self-absorbed or setting your mind on things of this earth, try fasting from it for a period (for example, two weeks or a month).

As you fast, examine your heart. Is it extremely difficult for you to fast from this form of media? That in itself is a sign that maybe it

---

13. John Owen, *The Mortification of Sin: Abridged and Made Easy to Read*, ed. Richard Rushing (Edinburgh: Banner of Truth, 2007), 85.

was taking up a little too much time and space in your life and mind. Are there certain areas of temptation in your life that are less threatening because this media is out of your life? Maybe cutting it out for good is a sacrifice you can make that will glorify God and bring you freedom from a particular sin.

After your period of fasting is over, you might find that your craving for that type of media is no longer as strong and you don't feel the need to add it back into your life. If you do add it back, continue to pay attention to how it impacts you. Were you drawn closer to God while it was out of your life? Or are you drawn closer to Him now that it is back in your life? What fruit was produced in your life when you cut it out? What fruit is being produced now that you've added it back in? It might not be sinful, but is it helpful to your spiritual life (1 Cor. 10:23)? Does it encourage you to set your mind on things above or on things here below?

This does not mean we can never consume media that is not explicitly Christian. But it does mean that when it comes to all forms of media, we desperately need wisdom from God and the fruit of self-control that comes from walking by the Spirit. Pray to God for wisdom (He promises He will give it), and then listen to the Spirit. When you feel a conviction in your conscience that aligns with the word of God so that you realize a specific form of media is not what you should be consuming right now to grow in the knowledge and grace of God, obey! That's taking a step by the Spirit. Taking step after step according to the Spirit is walking by the Spirit. Walking by the Spirit is what leads to the fruit of the Spirit, which includes self-control.

We often get this backward. We think that we need self-control in order to fast from certain forms of media. But self-control is a fruit of fasting, not a requirement for it. It is what grows when we take step after step according to the Spirit. Do you feel a lack of self-control in the area of media consumption? Then don't silence those Spirit-given convictions of conscience. Simply take the next step according to the Spirit, by His power, and for His glory, and then take another step, and another. That is what the Israelites did when they walked around

Jericho, and it is what you are called to do in this moment. Steps taken in obedience to God are guaranteed to lead to victory.

Cut It Out Completely

If fasting from a specific form of media for a time leads us to realize that it is linked to a particular sin in our lives, we must be willing to cut it out of our lives completely. It's not worth it to cling to any type of music, movie, novel, app, or website that is triggering sinful thoughts and putting you directly on the on-ramp to the highway of habitual sin. Like Joseph when Potiphar's wife approached him, flee the instant you realize what is happening (Gen. 39:12). Resist the devil by not giving him the opportunity to access your mind and soul through that website or movie. Know your weaknesses, know where you are prone to sin, and ruthlessly cut out sources of temptation.

When it comes to food, one of my weaknesses is chocolate. The easiest way for me to avoid eating too much chocolate is to leave it at the store. When I can muster enough willpower to pass the candy section in the grocery store without putting any chocolate in my cart, then I don't need willpower every time I walk past the cupboards in my kitchen because there isn't anything inside them to tempt me. Similarly, the easiest way to cut out a form of media that is leading you to sin is to make it impossible or extremely inconvenient to access it. That might mean setting up an internet blocker or having a friend change a password on your social media account. These types of actions taken before you are in the grip of temptation can be the "way of escape" that 1 Corinthians 10:13 mentions: "No temptation has overtaken you except such as is common to man; but God is faithful, who will not allow you to be tempted beyond what you are able, but with the temptation will also make the way of escape, that you may be able to bear it."

Another way I can avoid eating too much chocolate is to not eat it in private. The presence of other people while I am eating is a good deterrent for overeating. Having people around is also a good deterrent for sinning. Secrecy is to sin what oxygen is to fire. It is fuel. Remove it, and sin will die much more quickly. This might mean moving a computer out of a bedroom and into a public space in the home or asking a mature Christian to check in with you weekly and hold you accountable.

Whatever the particular sin or form of media is that we struggle with individually, we must be strategic about either limiting it or cutting it out completely. We can do this with God's help by asking and by following through on the three questions listed in the following table:

What sin am I prone to?	What media is feeding this sin?	How can I limit or cut out this media?
Materialism	Sales emails	Unsubscribe or set up a filter to send those emails to a separate folder.
Sexual sin	Sensual movies or shows	Use an internet filter or get rid of your video streaming service.
Wasting time	Social media	Ask a friend or family member to change your password for a set time.

Sin is no joke to God, and we must take it seriously. Limit or cut out whatever is drawing you away from God and closer to the world. "But put on the Lord Jesus Christ, and make no provision for the flesh, to fulfill its lusts" (Rom. 13:14).

Fill Up on the Good Stuff

While fasting from and cutting out certain forms of media, let's not forget that we need to be filling up on healthy nutrition. We will not grow if all we do is cut out junk food. We must replace it by consuming what will help us be as healthy and holy as possible—the Bible. This should be our focus even more than on what we cut out. What we fill our minds with is what God will use to renew our minds. Joel Beeke and Paul Smalley write,

The Bible is a pure source of truth, like a fountain of pure water in a world where all other sources have been contaminated by harmful substances and the activity of corrupt humanity. If we believe this, then we will drink deeply of the Holy Scriptures, and as little as possible of the lies of this world. Many people foolishly mingle the Word with vast quantities of worldly wisdom in their minds…. They give worldly media an equal or greater place in their lives in comparison to the Bible. It should not surprise us when worldliness chokes out the Word, so that it bears no fruit in such people (Mark 4:18–19).[14]

This is not about a restrictive diet enforced by the God who wants to cut all the fun out of our lives. This is about a nutritious feast offered by the God who wants us to grow up into the fruitful, Christlike people we were meant to be. J. Alasdair Groves and Winston T. Smith write, "Reading your Bible regularly over the years will make you a different person. Choosing to let Scripture's songs, sermons, and stories enter your mind is like choosing to eat a balanced, healthy diet: every cell in your body will be affected by access to good nutrients, mostly in ways you're never aware of."[15]

Do we want our lives to glorify God by producing fruit? Then we must remember that what we consume shapes who we are. If we want to be more like Jesus, we must look to Him and listen to His word. We might not crave that yet, but if we focus on future health by consuming Scripture regardless of whether we feel like it or not and by fasting from or cutting out worldly media, God promises that He will work in our minds and hearts. Seek, and you will find (Matt. 7:7). Eat, and you will live (John 6:51). Proper nutrition is essential to growth as a Christian, and God has given us everything that we need in His word and by His Spirit.

---

14. Joel R. Beeke and Paul M. Smalley, *Reformed Systematic Theology*, vol. 1, *Revelation and God* (Wheaton, Ill.: Crossway, 2019), 380–81.
15. Groves and Smith, *Untangling Emotions*, 126.

3

THINK

"All aboard!" A noisy plastic train chugs along the tracks my kids set up in our living room this morning. It bumps into a curved red piece of track and turns, continuing down the track that stretches to the left. Just before the train falls off the end of the track, my daughter grabs it and sets it down at the beginning to go again. She rushes to the red piece and turns it. Once again, the clanging train bumps into the red piece, but because my daughter turned it, this time the train rotates to the right and chugs cheerily into the station.

Our thoughts are like this train. They tend to chug along the same well-worn tracks over and over. One thought leads to another in a way that feels automatic and unstoppable, uncontrollable, unchangeable. It isn't often that we stop and consider that we can (and must!) control and manage our thought life. This is what God commands. It is not easy, but it is possible for the Christian by the power of the Holy Spirit. Like the plastic train, our trains of thought can be turned with the use of a barricade to block off negative, unholy tracks and point us in a more positive, holy direction.

That barricade is the word of God, which God uses to change our thoughts and renew our minds. When we purposefully bring to mind the knowledge and follow the commands given to us in the Bible, our thoughts are rerouted in a different direction. When we replace sinful thoughts by reciting verses, preaching truth to ourselves, and reminding ourselves that we do believe and what we believe, we end up in a different place. What we think, say, do, feel, and desire begins to change. Sinclair Ferguson explains, "As we allow the way we think and feel to be influenced by God's Word, our own responses to emerging situations will become increasingly moulded by the mind and will of God. As we live in his presence, we will become more like him; we will instinctively begin to think in a biblical, that is a godly, way about people and circumstances. We will begin to 'feel' about them in a way that expresses the attitude of God's own heart."[1]

After all, this is how God created us. He created our minds to develop patterns of thought, which allows us to do habitual tasks on autopilot, freeing us to think deeper thoughts than trying to remember how to brush our teeth or drive our cars. He also made our minds so that our patterns of thought are changeable. When we choose whether or not to pay attention to specific thoughts, our brains are physically changed. W. Yount explains, "The brain obediently goes where the mind leads, mechanically wiring what the mind attends."[2] Because we are sinful, our minds lead us along patterns of thought that are not holy. After we are saved, we need a way for our minds to be renewed so that our patterns of thought become more Christlike. That way is offered by the Holy Spirit working through the word of God. God has given us a variety of instructions about what and how to think. Since He is our Creator, these instructions line up perfectly with how we are created. It only makes sense to follow them if we want our minds to be renewed. Let's look at some of these instructions to discover what they actually mean and how we put them into practice.

Know: Be Still and Know

No matter what a person wants to put into practice, their mind must take in knowledge first. This is true for our spiritual lives as well. Before we can do anything, we must follow what God commands in Psalm 46:10: "Be still, and know that I am God." Knowledge of who

---

1. Ferguson, *Let's Study Philippians*, 15.
2. W. Yount, *Created to Learn: A Christian Teacher's Introduction to Education Psychology*, 2nd ed. (Nashville: B&H Academic, 2010), 537.

God is can be found in the Bible. God chose every word intentionally to convey the knowledge He wants us to have—the knowledge that He uses to renew our minds and transform our lives (Prov. 2:1–12). And every day we have the opportunity to pursue that knowledge or to leave it sitting dusty and untouched on the coffee table while we gorge ourselves on the knowledge of the world through a flickering screen. Which knowledge we seek will change our brains, renew our minds, and transform our lives, making us either more like Christ or more like the world.

Knowledge of any kind will change our brains. Research shows "that in fact the brain never stops changing through learning. Plasticity is the capacity of the brain to change with learning. Changes associated with learning occur mostly at the level of connections between neurons: New connections form and the internal structure of the existing synapses change."[3] In other words, what we learn literally changes the physical structure of our brains. It is critical to be incredibly careful about what knowledge we are taking in and thinking about.

Knowledge does not just change our brains; it is also what God uses to renew our minds. Depending on what kinds of knowledge we are consuming, different thoughts seem to automatically come to mind in different situations. The more we are regularly consuming the word of God, the more our automatic thought response is biblical. We recognize this in other people when they always have a verse or a hymn that comes to mind in any given conversation. If we want this to be true of us, we too must spend time consuming the knowledge that we want to be renewed by.

It's not just verses and hymns that come to mind when God is renewing our minds through knowledge. The knowledge we take in also shapes our entire mindset and worldview. As our minds are saturated with God's word and as we live in obedience to it, our mental reactions and trains of thought change entirely. Circumstances that

---

3. Pascale Michelon, "Brain Plasticity: How Learning Changes Your Brain," *Sharp Brains*, February 26, 2008, https://sharpbrains.com/blog/2008/02/26/brain-plasticity-how-learning-changes-your-brain/.

used to cue worry begin to cue thoughts about God being in control and caring for us. Temptations that used to cue sinful thoughts begin to cue an urgent fleeing of our minds to God in prayer. Other people who used to cue annoyance or anger begin to cue love. Information that used to cue disappointment begins to cue our minds to think about our eternal hope of being with Jesus in heaven. Even nature begins to cue certain verses and biblical principles, such as God caring for the birds and the righteous man being like a tree planted by the river. These changes in our minds are a result of God working through the knowledge we find in His word to renew our minds, strengthening the biblical paths of thought in our brains and weakening the sinful paths.

The natural result of God using knowledge to change our brains and renew our minds is that our lives are transformed. Knowledge strongly influences what we say and do, so it is important to pursue the knowledge that will lead to right and holy action. We see this in several of Paul's letters when he connects knowledge with action:

> And this I pray, that your love may abound still more and more in *knowledge* and all discernment, that you may approve the things that are excellent, that you may be sincere and without offense till the day of Christ, being filled with the fruits of righteousness which are by Jesus Christ, to the glory and praise of God. (Phil. 1:9–11)

> For this reason we also, since the day we heard it, do not cease to pray for you, and to ask that you may be filled with the *knowledge* of His will in all wisdom and spiritual understanding; that you may walk worthy of the Lord, fully pleasing Him, being fruitful in every good work and increasing in the *knowledge* of God. (Col. 1:9–10)

Paul goes on to tell the Colossians, "You have put off the old man with his deeds, and have put on the new man who is *renewed in knowledge* according to the image of Him who created him" (Col. 3:9–10). This is how God works: through knowledge freely offered in His word of who He is and what He desires that He uses to change who we are and what we desire. Joel Beeke and Paul Smalley write:

Christ's words imply that the knowledge of God illuminates the minds of men and guides their lives (John 1:4; 8:12), engages their faith in Christ (3:15–16; 6:47), delivers them from perdition (3:15–16; 10:28), releases them from condemnation (3:36; 5:24), satisfies their deepest desires (4:14; 6:35), brings them into communion with the living God (5:26), and guarantees their future resurrection to eternal life (6:40; 11:25). What a marvelous gift is the knowledge of God through Jesus Christ![4]

The more we use this gift of knowledge, the greater our view of and trust in God becomes. The more we trust Him, the more we will believe and ponder the knowledge He gives and the more our minds will be renewed and our lives transformed. Consume this knowledge like your life depends on it—because it does.

Meditate: Think about These Things

Once we have a base of knowledge, what should we do with it? The answer can be found in what is perhaps the most well-known instruction related to our thought life: "Whatsoever things are true, whatsoever things are honest, whatsoever things are just, whatsoever things are pure, whatsoever things are lovely, whatsoever things are of good report; if there be any virtue, and if there be any praise, think on these things" (Phil. 4:8 KJV). If this verse were lived out as much as it is quoted, we would all be further along in our sanctification. But it is difficult to live it out, especially if the information we are looking at and listening to fits the opposite description better: untrue, dishonest, unjust, impure, unlovely, of bad report, without virtue, without praise.

The most efficient way to make it easier to think on the things listed in this verse is to change what we are taking in through our eyes and ears. If we truly desire to think on these things, then we must be taking in information that helps us do so. How do we do this? What fits this description? Read the following verses from

---

4. Beeke and Smalley, *Reformed Systematic Theology*, 1:510–11.

Psalm 19:7–11 and notice how the italicized words mesh with the description in Philippians 4:8:

> The law of the LORD is *perfect*, converting the soul;
> The testimony of the LORD is *sure*, making wise the simple;
> The statutes of the LORD are *right*, rejoicing the heart;
> The commandment of the LORD is *pure*, enlightening the eyes;
> The fear of the LORD is *clean*, enduring forever;
> The judgments of the LORD are *true* and *righteous* altogether.
> More to be *desired* are they than gold,
> Yea, than much fine gold;
> *Sweeter* also than honey and the honeycomb.
> Moreover by them Your servant is warned,
> And in keeping them there is great reward.

It is the Word of God—both the physical copy of the Bible on your nightstand and the Word of God made flesh, Jesus Christ—that fits this description. But reading the Bible and learning about Jesus are only the first steps. Once we take in this information, the next step is to actually spend time thinking about it. It is through meditation that true, honest, just, pure, lovely, commendable, virtuous, praiseworthy things shape the way we think. It is no coincidence that David, a man after God's own heart, places so much emphasis on meditation: "I will meditate on Your precepts, and contemplate Your ways" (Ps. 119:15). "Oh, how I love Your law! It is my meditation all the day" (v. 97). He did not just happen to be a man after God's own heart. It was meditating on God's word and ways that shaped his heart—his thoughts, words, actions, feelings, and desires—to be more like God's.

But what exactly is meditation, and what effect does it have on our lives? J. I. Packer describes it as "the activity of calling to mind, and thinking over, and dwelling on, and applying to oneself, the various things that one knows about the works and ways and purposes and promises of God.... It is a matter of talking to oneself about God and oneself; it is, indeed, often a matter of arguing with oneself, reasoning oneself out of moods of doubt and unbelief into a clear apprehension of God's power and grace."[5]

Packer goes on to explain that the benefits of meditating are an increase in knowledge of God, peace, strength, and joy.[6] These are benefits we cannot expect to receive if we don't meditate. In Joshua 1:8, God tells Joshua, "This Book of the Law shall not depart from your mouth, but you shall meditate in it day and night, that you may observe to do according to all that is written in it. For then you will make your way prosperous, and then you will have good success." These effects are worth far more than the effort expended and should encourage us to make the time to meditate on Scripture. C. H. Spurgeon describes the inspiring result of meditation in the life of John Bunyan:

> It is blessed to eat into the very soul of the Bible until, at last, you come to talk in Scriptural language, and your very style is fashioned upon Scripture models, and, what is better still, your spirit is flavored with the words of the Lord. I would quote John Bunyan as an instance of what I mean. Read anything of his, and you will see that it is almost like reading the Bible itself.... Prick him anywhere; his blood is Bibline, the very essence of the Bible flows from him. He cannot speak without quoting a text, for his very soul is full of the Word of God.[7]

Meditation is also supported by modern scientific research as something that is healthy for our brains. Caroline Leaf writes, "When you go over and over something, reading it, thinking about it, writing it down, and then repeating this process, you deepen your knowledge and understanding, direct your attention, and grow nerve cells. The neurons in your brain line up and fire together because you are firing synapses over and over, which causes genetic expression to happen and makes the synapses and proteins stronger."[8]

5. Packer, *Knowing God*, 23.
6. Packer, *Knowing God*, 23.
7. *C. H. Spurgeon's Autobiography: Compiled from His Diary, Letters, and Records, by His Wife, and His Private Secretary* (1897–1999; repr., Pasadena, Tex.: Pilgrim Publications, 1992), 2:7.
8. Leaf, *Switch On Your Brain*, 108.

Despite the incredible spiritual and mental benefits, meditation does not come easily or naturally to most of us. It feels far more
natural to think about day-to-day matters, and it is easy to get so
wrapped up in our fast-paced lives that we never really make time
for meditation. Our busyness is slowly but surely leading us further
and further along a path that leads to death, not life. The Bible is full
of truths that have transforming power, but if we don't spend time
thinking about them, we will miss out. If we want our minds to be
renewed and our lives transformed, we must make time to *think* on
these things—for it is through thinking on these things that God
changes us. Seventeenth-century minister William Bridge explains
it plainly: "The more full your hand is of worldly employments, the
more you will think thereon; and the more you think thereon, the
less you will think of God and the things of God. And what is the
reason that many meditate and think so little of God and the things
of God, but because their hearts are so full of the world."[9]

This is where the lofty concept of meditation comes down to
simple, practical matters for many of us. Maybe our schedules are
too full or we need better strategies for time management or we are
simply spending too much time on things that don't matter at all.
Everything we consume, own, and do takes up space in our minds,
and the more we take in to our lives, the less time there is to think
about God's word. If we have so much going on that there is no time
to meditate, something needs to be cut out. John Owen writes, "How
can we say we love Christ and spiritual things if we do not spend
much time thinking about them? That which you set your heart on
is that which you will think about most."[10] And that which we think
about most will influence what our hearts are set on.

It could also be that we have time to meditate, but we aren't sure
where to begin or how to go about it. Here we can gain wisdom from
Christians of the past. In their book *Puritan Theology*, Joel Beeke and

---

9. William Bridge, "The Sweetness and Profitableness of Divine Meditation,"
in *The Works of Rev. William Bridge* (1845; repr., Beaver Falls, Pa.: Soli Deo Gloria,
1989), 3:132.

10. Owen, *Spiritual-Mindedness*, 238.

Mark Jones share several helpful practical guidelines offered by the Puritans for the process of meditation:

- Begin by asking the Holy Spirit for assistance.
- Read the Scriptures, then select a verse or doctrine upon which to meditate.
- Select subjects that are most applicable to your present circumstances.
- Memorize the selected verse(s), or some aspect of the subject.
- Fix your thoughts on the Scripture or a scriptural subject.
- Consider various aspects of your subject: its names, causes, qualities, fruits, and effect.
- Stir up affections, such as love, desire, hope, courage, gratitude, zeal, and joy, to glorify God.
- Apply your meditations to yourself, to arouse your soul to duty and comfort, and to restrain your soul from sin.
- Examine yourself for your own growth in grace.
- Turn your applications into resolutions.
- Conclude with prayer, thanksgiving, and psalm singing.
- Don't shift too quickly from meditation to engagement with things of this world.[11]

Are we willing to take the time to work through these steps in our devotional life, knowing that meditation will bring great benefits in our lives? Will we trade in some of our precious media accounts, belongings, or events for more time to think about God's word and ways? These sacrifices will be difficult to offer but can be made out of faith that God will work through the time we spend meditating to renew our minds and transform us into the image of Christ.

Focus: Set Your Mind on Things Above

Another verse about the mind that is often quoted is Colossians 3:2: "Set your mind on things above, not on things on the earth." This

---

11. Beeke and Jones, *Puritan Theology*, 897–99.

verse, too, is easier to quote than to live out, especially if we don't stop to think about what it really means. Sometimes the easiest way to figure out what a verse means is to first think about its opposite. What would it mean to set your mind on things on the earth? We can find out from several other verses in the Bible:

> Do not love the world or the things in the world. If anyone loves the world, the love of the Father is not in him. For all that is in the world—the lust of the flesh, the lust of the eyes, and the pride of life—is not of the Father but is of the world. And the world is passing away, and the lust of it; but he who does the will of God abides forever. (1 John 2:15–17)

> Brethren, join in following my example, and note those who so walk, as you have us for a pattern. For many walk, of whom I have told you often, and now tell you even weeping, that they are the enemies of the cross of Christ: whose end is destruction, whose god is their belly, and whose glory is in their shame—who set their mind on earthly things. (Phil. 3:17–19)

To set our minds on the things of earth, then, is to spend our thinking time focused on what our flesh desires, what our eyes desire, and what possessions we own or desire. When we spend most of our time thinking about these things, our minds become set on them and our lives become focused on attempts to satisfy these desires. What we think, say, and do becomes centered on our desires for food, money, possessions, sex, status, beauty, and comfort. We hardly realize that there is an entirely different, eternity-focused way of thinking and living.

An example of someone thinking in this earthly way is Peter in Matthew 16. Jesus had been talking about how He would suffer and die, and Peter told Jesus that these things would not happen to Him. For Peter the focus was avoiding suffering and death and holding on to comfort and life. He could not see the eternal result of Jesus's suffering and death because he was too focused on the things of earth. In verses 23–26, Jesus tells him,

"Get behind Me, Satan! You are an offense to Me, for you are not mindful of the things of God, but the things of man."

Then Jesus said to His disciples, "If anyone would come after Me, let him deny himself, and take up his cross, and follow Me. For whoever desires to save his life will lose it, but whoever loses his life for My sake will find it. For what profit is it to a man if he gains the whole world, and loses his own soul? Or what will a man give in exchange for his soul?"

Setting our minds on things of earth means that, like Peter, we think about our earthly desires for comfort and life so much that all our words and actions are aimed at fulfilling those desires, making us unwilling to give anything up in order to follow Jesus. But setting our minds on things above means we think about following Jesus so much that we value following Him more than fulfilling our earthly desires, making us willing to deny ourselves and lose our lives in order to follow. We see God's transforming power at work in Peter, as this became his mindset later in life when he wrote, "Therefore, since Christ suffered for us in the flesh, arm yourselves also with the same mind, for he who has suffered in the flesh has ceased from sin, that he no longer should live the rest of his time in the flesh for the lusts of men, but for the will of God" (1 Peter 4:1–2).

How did Peter's mindset change so drastically? The things above became more real to him than the things below. The same can be true for us over time as God works in our lives. The more we purposefully think about the things above, the more natural this way of thinking will become to us. Elisabeth Elliot describes this change: "The transformation of the mind produces a transformed vision of reality. What the world calls 'real' will lose its clarity. What it calls 'unreal' will gain clarity and power.... It is nothing short of a transformed vision of reality that is able to see Christ as more real than the storm, love more real than hatred, meekness more real than pride, long-suffering more real than annoyance, holiness more real than sin."[12]

---

12. Elliot, *Joyful Surrender*, 59–60.

The more time we spend in Scripture, in prayer, and in meditation on things above, the more our minds will be set on those things and the more real heaven and eternity will become to us. In his early eighteenth-century Bible commentary, Matthew Henry emphasizes, "We must mind the concerns of another world more than the concerns of this."[13] This requires effort and intention, but it is worth it because setting our minds on heavenly things transforms the entire focus of our lives. Another eighteenth-century theologian, Adam Clarke, writes, "Now, that ye are converted to God, act in reference to heavenly things as ye did formerly in reference to those of earth; and vice versa."[14] When our thinking changes, what we say and do changes. And when our words and actions change, God slowly but surely transforms our feelings and desires. As John Owen observes, "So when we by faith set our minds on those things which are above, where Christ sits at the right hand of God, then the things of earth lose their lustre and desirability in comparison."[15]

Is this happening in your life? Has your thinking shifted from a focus on fulfilling earthly desires to a focus on following Jesus? Have your words, actions, feelings, and desires been transformed as a result? If not, why not? Could it be that you simply have not tried to think more about heavenly things? Owen continues, "We lack skill and ability to think rightly about invisible things. But the way to learn is to get started."[16] Our transformation is God's work, but He works through our obedience to His commands: "Set your mind on things above" (Col. 3:2). And He promises great reward for obeying:

> You will keep him in perfect peace,
> Whose mind is stayed on You,
> Because he trusts in You. (Isa. 26:3)

---

13. *Matthew Henry's Commentary in One Volume* (Grand Rapids: Zondervan, 1961), 1872.

14. Adam Clarke, *Clarke's Commentary*, on Colossians 3:2, Bible Hub, accessed December 31, 2020, https://biblehub.com/commentaries/clarke/colossians/3.htm.

15. Owen, *Spiritual-Mindedness*, 49.

16. Owen, *Spiritual-Mindedness*, 49.

Capture: Bring Every Thought into Captivity

Setting our minds on things above and staying our minds on God requires every earthly thought to be brought into captivity to the obedience of Christ (2 Cor. 10:5). This verse is often misinterpreted as a command for each of us to bring our every sinful thought into captivity. Instead, according to John Piper, "it is a statement about what Paul is doing to his opponents. He is demolishing their world-view and then taking their defeated thoughts captive for Christ so that they become right thinkers—obedient in the way they think about Christ."[17]

So how do we apply it to our lives? By realizing that "the place we belong in is the group whose opinions and thoughts Paul is trying to demolish.... We should listen to Paul and submit all our thoughts and ideas and feelings about God and about life to Paul's teaching (as God's apostle) for scrutiny. And if anything is out of sync with Paul's teaching, we should let it be destroyed."[18] If we are to submit everything to what Paul and the rest of the biblical authors teach, then we must

- know what the Bible says,
- compare our thoughts to what it says,
- believe and live according to what it says instead of according to what we originally thought.

Practically, this means that we need to be reading our Bibles every day not just to check a duty off the list but to familiarize ourselves with truth. We must then use that truth every day, which will become easier as we become more familiar with it. We use the truth of the Bible by preaching it to ourselves in response to our earthly thoughts. As Martyn Lloyd-Jones writes, "Take yourself in hand, you have to address yourself, preach to yourself, question yourself.... And then you must go on to remind yourself of God, Who God is

---

17. John Piper, "How Do I Take My Thoughts Captive?," interview with John Piper, Ask Pastor John, March 3, 2015, podcast, https://www.desiringgod.org/interviews/how-do-i-take-my-thoughts-captive.
18. Piper, "How Do I Take My Thoughts Captive?"

and what God is and what God has done, and what God has pledged Himself to do."[19] To do this, we can put together "scripts" based on biblical truth that we "read through" in our thoughts every time our minds turn toward earthly thoughts. Because different people experience different struggles and temptations, these scripts will vary, but they must always be based on the infallible word of God. It may be helpful to physically write out your own scripts to preach to yourself to fight the specific earthly thoughts you struggle with most, but here are some examples to get you started.

Earthly Thoughts	Script to Preach to Yourself
Doubting God's goodness	God says He is good. Do I believe that? Yes, I do. God also says He works all things together for good to those who love Him (Rom. 8:28). Do I believe that? Yes. Do I love Him? Yes. Since I believe that He is good and that He works things together for good to those who love Him and I love Him, then these circumstances must be for my eternal good so that I can be conformed to the image of Christ (v. 29). They don't feel good right now, but I believe that God knows better than I do, that His vision is eternal where mine is only temporal. I trust Him more than I trust myself. Therefore I am thankful even for these hard circumstances because I know they are for my good (Ps. 119:71).
Struggling with worry	God says I should not be anxious about anything (Phil. 4:6). This instruction is hard for me to follow, but my worries are an opportunity to turn to God.[20] He tells me what to do instead of being anxious. He tells me to let Him know my requests by prayer and supplication with thanksgiving, and He promises that peace will be the result (vv. 6–7). Do I believe this promise? Yes. So instead of running

---

19. David Martyn Lloyd-Jones, *Spiritual Depression: Its Causes and Cure* (Grand Rapids: Eerdmans, 1964), 20–21.

20. Edward T. Welch, *When I Am Afraid* (Greensboro, N.C.: New Growth Press, 2010), 13.

Earthly Thoughts	Script to Preach to Yourself
	through my worries over and over, I will pray to God about them and thank God for any benefit I can find in this difficult situation, even if the only benefit I can find is that it is drawing me closer to God by increasing my prayer life.
Feeling discontentment	God says He supplies all my needs (Phil. 4:19) and has given me all things pertaining to life and godliness (2 Peter 1:3). There is still something that I desperately desire, but because of God's word, I know that to have this desired thing would not make me more like Jesus. I still want this thing, but more than this thing, I want to be like Jesus and I want to glorify God with my life. So I can pray like Jesus did in the garden, explaining what I want to God but then submitting that desire by praying that God's will, not mine, would be done (Luke 22:42). This is a prayer that God has promised He will answer (1 John 5:14–15).
Dreading trials	God says that He disciplines those He loves (Heb. 12:6) and that the discipline may feel painful now, but it will yield righteousness (v. 11). Do I believe this? Yes. I have disciplined my own children because I love them and want to train them in the way they should go, and I believe God does the same for me. Without these trials, I might have stayed satisfied with this world and never turned to God. Because of these trials, the world is no longer enough to distract or console me, and I must turn to God. Even in this trial, I can see my mind being trained to turn to God instead of the world, and that is a far greater blessing than any outward blessing (such as health or prosperity) that the world has to offer. God is making me more like Christ (Rom. 8:29) and preparing me for glory (2 Cor. 4:17–18)! I would not have it any other way.

Rejecting unbiblical thoughts and preaching truth to ourselves are not magic pills that instantly cure our sinful ways of thinking. They are habits that we must learn and practice day after day. Seventeenth-century Bible commentator John Trapp states, "If any ungodly or unjust thing shall be suggested to me…I will cast it out of my mind and thoughts with abhorrency."[21] We must do the same and then replace our thoughts with God's. Reformer John Calvin declares, "Oh, how greatly has the man advanced who has learned not to be his own, not to be governed by his own reason, but to surrender his mind to God!"[22] We were created to have minds that are surrendered to God, thinking His thoughts after Him. This is how God created our minds, and it is how we work best. As our minds are "marinated with Scripture,"[23] the Holy Spirit uses these truths to renew and transform us so that we begin to truly understand, do, and desire God's will (Rom. 12:2).

Memorize: Hide the Word in Your Heart

Thinking on these things, setting our minds on things above, and bringing our thoughts into captivity will be much easier if we are consistently working on hiding God's word in our hearts (Ps. 119:11) through memorizing Bible verses. God's truth must be stored in our brains first if we are going to store and treasure it in our hearts. It is memorization that provides material to think about and set our minds on during the hours of the day that we do not have a physical copy of the Bible in front of us.

Why is memorizing Scripture so important? God gives us many good reasons.

> The law of his God is in his heart; none of his steps shall slide. (Ps. 37:31)

> How can a young man keep his way pure? By guarding it according to your word. (Ps. 119:9 ESV)

> I will never forget Your precepts, for by them You have given me life. (Ps. 119:93)

---

21. John Trapp, *A Commentary on the Old and New Testaments*, ed. Hugh Martin (London: Richard D. Dickinson, 1868), 2:624.

22. As quoted in John Blanchard, *The Complete Gathered Gold: A Treasury of Quotations for Christians* (Darlington, England: Evangelical Press, 2007), 415.

23. Beeke and Smalley, *Reformed Systematic Theology*, 1:450.

If you abide in Me, and My words abide in you, you will ask what you desire, and it shall be done for you. (John 15:7)

Perhaps one of the main reasons we should be spending time memorizing Bible verses comes from Psalm 119:11: "Your word I have hidden in my heart, that I might not sin against You." Hiding God's word in our hearts is not just a nice thing to do. It is something we must do if we want to be able to fight against sin. It is a weapon to be used in our spiritual battles. It is how we can have "the sword of the Spirit, which is the word of God" (Eph. 6:17) not just sitting on our nightstands but accessible—in our minds to be unsheathed and used the moment temptation comes to us.

To understand how to use the Bible verses we have memorized to fight temptation, think of the example of Jesus in the wilderness in Matthew 4. Satan presented Him with three different temptations, and each time Jesus responded by quoting a verse from the Old Testament. When Satan tempted Him to turn stones to bread, He quoted Deuteronomy 8:3: "Man shall not live by bread alone, but by every word that proceeds from the mouth of God" (Matt. 4:4). When Satan tempted Jesus to throw Himself down from the pinnacle of the temple, he quoted Scripture to get Jesus to fall, but Jesus responded by quoting Deuteronomy 6:16: "You shall not tempt the LORD your God" (Matt. 4:7). When Satan tempted Jesus to bow down to him, Jesus replied by quoting Deuteronomy 6:13: "You shall worship the LORD your God, and Him only you shall serve" (Matt. 4:10).

As we consider Jesus's responses, we must remember that He was human as well as divine. This means that these intense temptations were not easy for Him to resist. And so He pulled out His best weapon to fight Satan and sin: the word of God, likely memorized when He was younger, pulled from His memory, and spoken aloud in the midst of the battle. If this was Jesus's best weapon, then we cannot ask for a better weapon against temptation. But are we using it? Are we selecting verses that will help us fight the specific sins that we struggle with the most? Are we committing these verses to memory and bringing them to mind or speaking them out loud when we are in the middle of the battle? Reformer Martin Luther says, "When the flesh begins to cut up the only remedy is to take the sword of the Spirit, the word of salvation, and fight against the flesh. If you set the Word out of sight, you are helpless against the flesh. I know this to be a fact. I have been assailed by many violent passions, but as soon as I took hold of some Scripture passage, my temptations left me. Without the Word I could not have helped myself against the flesh."[24]

The Holy Spirit will work through His word, stored in our minds and hearts, to give us the strength to fight the battle, and the way we respond to temptation will change. Our swords are sitting on our nightstands. It's time to unsheathe them and use them in daily life. It's time to follow Jesus into the battle and copy the strategy He used to fight.

Remember: Recall the Deeds of the Lord

Bible verses are not the only thing we should be committing to memory and playing over and over again in our minds. It is also helpful in our spiritual walk of faith to remember and replay the ways God has worked in the past (Isa. 46:9)—in our personal lives, in the lives of our friends and family, in church history, and especially on the cross. According to Rick Renner, "We should constantly hit the rewind button in our minds and 'replay' the times that God has been faithful to us in the past...until we never forget His faithfulness to us!"[25] Remembering and replaying evidence of God's faithfulness strengthens our faith, worship, witness, and hope.

First, *remembering strengthens our faith*. In Psalm 143, David was overwhelmed and distressed, but his response to those feelings was,

> I remember the days of old;
> I meditate on all Your works;
> I muse on the work of Your hands. (v. 5)

---

24. Martin Luther, as quoted in David Guzik, "Study Guide for Galatians 5," Study Resources: Text Commentaries, Blue Letter Bible, https://www.blueletterbible.org/Comm/guzik_david/StudyGuide2017-Gal/Gal-5.cfm.
25. Rick Renner, *Sparkling Gems from the Greek* (Tulsa, Okla.: Harrison House), 1:6.

When he looked back on how God had worked in his life, he could see that God had a track record of faithfulness, and his faith was strengthened. Asaph had the same response in Psalm 77. The psalm starts with him in anguish, questioning God, but then he focused his mind on remembering what God had done:

> Will the Lord cast off forever?
> And will He be favorable no more?
> Has His mercy ceased forever?
> Has His promise failed forevermore?
> Has God forgotten to be gracious?
> Has He in anger shut up His tender mercies? Selah
>
> And I said, "This is my anguish;
> But I will remember the years of the right hand of the
>   Most High."
> I will remember the works of the LORD;
> Surely I will remember Your wonders of old.
> I will also meditate on all Your work,
> And talk of Your deeds. (Ps. 77:7–12)

It was remembering, meditating, and talking about God's works that turned Asaph from anguished, doubting questioning to hopeful, faith-filled declaration. Remembering, meditating, and talking about how God has worked in our lives and brought us through temptations and trials can strengthen our faith too.

Second, *remembering strengthens our worship.* Psalm 107 paints several different pictures of God delivering His people from various perils. In each situation, "they cried out to the LORD in their trouble," and He saved or delivered "them out of their distresses" (vv. 6, 13, 19, 28). And each time the Lord saved them, the psalmist expresses his desire "that men would give thanks to the LORD for His goodness, and for His wonderful works to the children of men!" (Ps. 107:8, 15, 21, 31). When we remember God's goodness to us in the past, true worship comes more readily.

Third, *remembering strengthens our witness.* This was especially prevalent among the Old Testament Israelites, who often built altars as a way of remembering specific places where God met them, blessed them, and made promises to them. These altars gave them the opportunity to explain to others, including their own children, how God had worked in the past (Josh. 4:20–24). We may not build altars today, but we can use this principle by sharing with others the ways God has worked in our lives through conversation, writing, or music. We hear an example of this in "My Song Forever Shall Record," based on Psalm 89:

> My song forever shall record
> The tender mercies of the Lord;
> Thy faithfulness will I proclaim,
> And every age shall know Thy Name.
>
> I sing of mercies that endure,
> Forever builded firm and sure,
> Of faithfulness that never dies,
> Established changeless in the skies.[26]

Finally, *remembering strengthens our hope*. In Lamentations 3:21–23, we read,

> This I recall to my mind,
> *Therefore* I have hope.
>
> Through the LORD's mercies we are not consumed,
> Because His compassions fail not.
> They are new every morning;
> Great is Your faithfulness.

Hope grows when we remember past evidence of God's faithfulness and use it to strengthen our belief that He will fulfill His promises of future faithfulness. He has done it before. He will do it again.

---

26. *The Psalter, with Doctrinal Standards, Liturgy, Church Order, and Added Chorale Section* (1965; repr., Grand Rapids: Eerdmans for Reformation Heritage Books, 2003), 241:1–2.

Hope: Look at the Things Which Are Not Seen

As much as the Bible talks about remembering the past, it is also very future focused. In 2 Corinthians 4:16–18, we read,

> We do not lose heart. Even though our outward man is perishing, yet the inward man is being renewed day by day. For our light affliction, which is but for a moment, is working for us a far more exceeding and eternal weight of glory, while we do not look at the things which are seen, but at the things which are not seen. For the things which are seen are temporary, but the things which are not seen are eternal.

Spending time thinking about our eternal future—entering glory; seeing Jesus for the first time; hearing Him say, "Well done"; worshiping God with countless others; speaking with other saints; staying in the place prepared for us; knowing the joy of sinless perfection—these are the thoughts that bring joy and motivation to our life here on earth. Spurgeon writes:

> See, then, the happy estate of a Christian! He has his best things last, and he therefore in this world receives his worst things first. But even his worst things are "afterward" good things, harsh ploughings yielding joyful harvests. Even now he grows rich by his losses, he rises by his falls, he lives by dying, and becomes full by being emptied; if, then, his grievous afflictions yield him so much peaceable fruit in this life, what shall be the full vintage of joy "afterwards" in heaven? If his dark nights are as bright as the world's days, what shall his days be? If even his starlight is more splendid than the sun, what must his sunlight be?[27]

Yet so many of us don't take advantage of the hope of a joyful "afterward" because we don't use our minds to think about our eternal future very often. We do, of course, think about future temporal things. For example, when we have a vacation planned in a few weeks, we spend time imagining the break from our daily tasks and relaxing with our families. Thinking about vacation gives us

---

27. Spurgeon, *Morning and Evening*, 295.

motivation to prepare for vacation. We work on packing what we will need and finishing up the work that should be completed before we go. Everything else fades to the background and seems to matter less. All this increases our anticipation and hope for the week when we will finally be on vacation.

Thinking about eternity also increases joy, hope, and motivation but to a far greater extent than thinking about a mere vacation. Paul gives a notable example in 2 Timothy 4:6–8: "For I am already being poured out as a drink offering, and the time of my departure is at hand. I have fought the good fight, I have finished the race, I have kept the faith. Finally, there is laid up for me the crown of righteousness, which the Lord, the righteous Judge, will give to me on that Day, and not to me only but also to all who have loved His appearing." Jesus Himself was able to endure the horrors of the cross because He had hope in "the joy that was set before Him" (Heb. 12:2). Although none of us have to endure as much as He did, we can follow His example and use the promises of the Bible and the joy it sets before us to endure in this temporary life. The following chart helps us see what gives hope for an eternal future with Christ and how that hope helps us today.

What Gives Hope?	What Is the Result of That Hope?	Reference
We think about how God will still help us and we will yet praise Him.	We are no longer so cast down and disquieted.	Psalm 42
We think about how we are surrounded by a great cloud of witnesses.	We lay aside every distraction and sin which clings so closely.	Hebrews 12:1
We think about how Jesus endured the cross because of the joy set before Him.	We run with endurance the race that is set before us.	Hebrews 12:1–2

What Gives Hope?	What Is the Result of That Hope?	Reference
We think about how God disciplines those He loves and how discipline yields righteousness even though it feels painful for the moment.	We struggle against sin, endure through discipline, and feel encouraged.	Hebrews 12:3–13
We think about the positive outcome of the conduct of faithful Christians.	We follow the way they live.	Hebrews 13:7
We think about salvation through Jesus and put on the hope of salvation as a helmet.	We encourage and build up one another.	1 Thessalonians 5:8
We think about how trustworthy God is and how He saves those who believe.	We are willing to labor and suffer reproach for the cause of the gospel.	1 Timothy 4:10
We think about how Jesus will come again and how He gave Himself for us to redeem us.	We deny ungodliness and worldly lusts, and we live in a sober, righteous, and godly way.	Titus 2:11–14
We think about the grace that will be brought to us when Christ comes again.	We don't conform to our former lusts but strive for holiness in all our conduct.	1 Peter 1:13–16

Why are there so many verses that link promises about God and our eternal future with how we should live today? Because spending time thinking about these promises increases our hope, and that hope naturally leads to action. God did not have to let us know about our eternal, glorious future, but He did. Use this gift! Use His promises to inspire you today. Imagine eternity. Think about what comes afterward. Really believe that something better is coming. Think about that better future thing more than you think about your present circumstances. Your hope for the future will fuel your efforts in godliness today. Never forget that today's afflictions are preparing you for an eternal weight of glory beyond anything you can imagine. First Peter 1:3–9 sums it up well:

> Blessed be the God and Father of our Lord Jesus Christ, who according to His abundant mercy has begotten us again to a living hope through the resurrection of Jesus Christ from the dead, to an inheritance incorruptible and undefiled and that does not fade away, reserved in heaven for you, who are kept by the power of God through faith for salvation ready to be revealed in the last time.
>
> In this you greatly rejoice, though now for a little while, if need be, you have been grieved by various trials, that the genuineness of your faith, being much more precious than gold that perishes, though it is tested by fire, may be found to praise, honor, and glory at the revelation of Jesus Christ, whom having not seen you love. Though now you do not see Him, yet believing, you rejoice with joy inexpressible and full of glory, receiving the end of your faith—the salvation of your souls.

It is only by thinking according to the word of God that we can have this hope and feel this joy that Peter expresses. If we keep on thinking the way we have always thought, our minds will not be renewed. But if we, by the power of the Spirit, use the word of God as a barricade against our natural sinful way of thinking, He will put us on the right track toward a positive, holy way of thinking. And so we must grow in knowledge of God and His word, not just skimming it but meditating deeply on it; set our minds on eternity instead of this world, preaching biblical truths to ourselves to replace unbiblical thinking; memorize verses so that we can fight sin and focus on God even when our Bibles are not physically open in front of us; and remember God's past faithfulness so that we can have a certain hope that He will fulfill what He has promised for the future. This is how God renews minds and transforms lives.

4

SAY AND DO

Waiting in the long lines at the secretary of state office seems to bring out the worst in all of us. Several years ago, while waiting rather impatiently for my number to be called, I overheard two women complaining that the numbers being called were totally random and that there was no order or logic to the system. Assuming there must be some sort of order, I began to pay more attention and soon realized that those of us who were waiting had been handed two different sets of numbers—probably devoted to different types of requests—and that certain desks were assigned to either set. Knowing this, I could understand why forty-eight had been followed by ten, forty-nine, and eleven. I began to wait more patiently and no longer felt the urge to voice my complaints with the others. Because my thoughts had changed, I spoke and acted differently than I would have otherwise.

This example is a trivial one. Thinking about how the secretary of state office has a logical system to handle their lines does not have much of an impact on daily life. But thinking about God does. Consuming God's word and thinking according to it make a visible difference in our lives because God uses our changed minds to bring about a change in our words and actions. What we consume and what we think transforms what we say and do. Michael Barrett observes, "Right thinking about the gospel produces right living in the gospel."[1]

---

1. Barrett, *Complete in Him*, 195.

This connection is especially clear in the writings of Paul. In his letters to various churches, the pattern that he often uses is to first explain how his readers should think and then how they should live as a result of that thinking. Ferguson explains, "He wants to train his readers to think Christianly in order that they may live faithfully."[2] Paul tells us that when we grow in knowledge from the word of God (Col. 3:9–10) and behold God (2 Cor. 3:18), our minds are being renewed. In other words, we begin to think different, more holy thoughts. As our minds are renewed, we are more and more able to discern the will of God (Rom. 12:2). This is important because it is only by discerning God's will that we are able to walk in a manner worthy of the Lord (Col. 1:9–10) by putting off the old man and putting on the new man (Eph. 4:20–24; Col. 3:9–10). Walking in this manner pleases God and gives us life and peace (Rom. 8:5–8). What we say and do is different than it used to be because our thoughts are different than they used to be. Our lives have been and continue to be transformed by the renewing of our minds. Rob Moll points out, "Paul clearly saw that internal change comes hand in hand with external change. For Paul, and for neuroscientists who study brain activity today, the connection between what we think and what we do is a powerful one."[3]

This principle of connecting thought and action is not found just in Paul's letters. We find the same idea in the Old Testament when we study the word *shema*. It is a word that can be translated as "hear" or "obey" (Ex. 19:5; Deut. 6:3–6; Isa. 55:3). A video from the BibleProject explains its meaning:

> When God asks the people to *shema*, what He means is that they listen *and* obey.... In ancient Hebrew, there is no separate word for obey.... Listening and doing are two sides of the same coin.... The Israelites of course could hear just fine, but they weren't actually listening or else they would act differently.... Real listening takes effort *and* action.[4]

---

2. Ferguson, *Let's Study Philippians*, 106.
3. Moll, *What Your Body Knows about God*, 30–31.
4. BibleProject, "Shema—Listen," March 24, 2017, written and directed by Jon Collins and Tim Mackie, video, https://www.youtube.com/watch?v=6KQLOuIKaRA.

This is how God created us. What we hear, what we see, and what we think as a result of hearing and seeing cannot help but bring about change in what we say and do. Jesus remarks, "My mother and My brothers are these who hear the word of God and do it" (Luke 8:21). Joel Beeke and Paul Smalley write, "In the biblical perspective, we have not heard God rightly unless we do what he says."[5] What we think and what we believe is how we'll live,[6] and so our prayer must be,

> Teach me your way, O LORD,
>   that I may walk in your truth;
>   unite my heart to fear your name.
>   (Ps. 86:11 ESV)

This chapter will explore the connection between what we think and what we say and do. We will see how our words and actions both reveal our thoughts and influence how we think. Then we will look at specific examples of truths to think about and how spending time thinking about those truths transforms what we say and do.

What You Say and Do Reveals What You Think

Imagine walking into the office of a financial advisor. You sit down together, and he pulls out some paperwork showing various graphs relating to a specific investment fund. As you look at these papers, he talks to you about how investing your money in this fund would be a wonderful opportunity. As you listen to him, you think through whether or not you should invest, and you come to a conclusion in your mind. Your advisor, however, does not know your conclusion until you tell him what it is and take action on it—either you sign the papers to commit to investing or you walk out the door without signing. Either way, what you say and do has provided clear evidence of what you think and believe.

---

5. Beeke and Smalley, *Reformed Systematic Theology*, 1:139.
6. Joel Beeke, "How Can I Help My Family Overcome Worldliness?" (sermon, Heritage Reformed Congregation, Grand Rapids, Mich., June 16, 2019), https://www.sermonaudio.com/sermoninfo.asp?SID=61519154591583.

When it comes to believing in God and His word, the same principle applies. We look at and listen to God and His word, and we have certain thoughts in response. What we say and do provides evidence of what those thoughts are, whether they are thoughts of belief or thoughts of doubt. If they are thoughts of doubt, we may end up ignoring God's word, moving on quickly to thoughts of other things. But if they are thoughts of belief, we begin to respond to God and His word differently than we did before. What we say and do changes over time to align more and more with what God wants us to say and do. In other words, we begin to obey Him. The Bible is full of this expectation that when we believe—when there is a change in our thinking—there ought to be a change in our response. What we say and do reveals what is in our hearts and minds, and if God has given us new hearts and is renewing our minds, our words and actions ought to be transformed. As John Stott asserts, "The secret to holy living is in the mind."[7] Obedience is the natural result of a mind that is being renewed. This is made clear in many verses:

> And you shall remember that the LORD your God led you all the way these forty years in the wilderness, to humble you and test you, to know what was in your heart, whether you would keep His commandments or not. (Deut. 8:2)

> I, the LORD, search the heart,
> I test the mind,
> Even to give every man according to his ways,
> According to the fruit of his doings. (Jer. 17:10)

> For a good tree does not bear bad fruit, nor does a bad tree bear good fruit. For every tree is known by its own fruit. For men do not gather figs from thorns, nor do they gather grapes from a bramble bush. A good man out of the good treasure of his heart brings forth good; and an evil man out of the evil treasure of his heart brings forth evil. For out of the abundance of the heart his mouth speaks. (Luke 6:43–45)

---

7. As quoted in Blanchard, *Complete Gathered Gold*, 416.

If you know these things, blessed are you if you do them. (John 13:17)

But be doers of the word, and not hearers only, deceiving yourselves. (James 1:22)

What we think in response to God's word has a powerful influence over what we say and do on a daily basis. We are constantly being presented with a variety of information, circumstances, and temptations. What we say and do in response to all this input reveals what we are thinking. Joel Beeke and Mark Jones write, "We can only live as Christians in the present evil age if we have the mind of Christ, that is, if we are genuinely heavenly minded, seeing our earth and this age from the perspective of heaven."[8] If our thoughts about the Bible are choked out by "the cares of this world, the deceitfulness of riches, and the desires for other things" (Mark 4:19), there will be no fruit to show. Our disobedience and lack of fruit will prove that we are thinking like the world. If, however, we "hear the word" and "accept it," aligning our thoughts with it, we will "bear fruit" (v. 20). We will be like the new Christians in Acts who, as a result of receiving the word, increased in learning, fellowship, prayer, hospitality, generosity, joy, and worship (Acts 2:41–47). We will obey God, and our obedience will reveal what is in our hearts and provide evidence that our minds are being renewed.

What You Say and Do Influences What You Think

A renewed mind necessarily leads to transformed words and actions. But the connection goes the other way too. What we say and do has influence over our thoughts. Romans 8:5 says, "For those who live according to the flesh set their minds on the things of the flesh, but those who live according to the Spirit, the things of the Spirit." When we find our minds spiraling into thought patterns that are more according to the flesh than to the Spirit, what we say and do can either lead us deeper into those spirals or help shake us out of them and

---

8. Beeke and Jones, *Puritan Theology*, 902.

realign our thoughts with what God teaches us. John Owen wrote about how our words and actions affect our spiritual-mindedness: "When men are careless and do not keep a watch over their hearts; when they neglect holy duties; when they are strangers to meditation on holy things and to self-examination; when they spend much time chasing after the world; when they will not endure hardship for Christ, it is useless to expect them to thrive and grow in grace and in spiritual-mindedness."[9]

How can we apply this principle in our lives? God has given us many practices, called spiritual disciplines, through which He renews our minds by increasing our spiritual-mindedness. These disciplines include reading the Bible, prayer, worship, evangelism, serving, stewardship, fasting, silence and solitude, journaling, and learning.[10] They are ways of speaking and acting that sometimes feel pointless because they rarely produce immediate results. But it helps us to stay motivated if we think of them as exercise. Someone who goes out for a jog often ends up in the same location where she started, more tired than she was before. If her goals are to go somewhere else or to have more energy immediately, jogging would not be the right choice. She might as well drive. But if her goals are increased muscle, health, and long-term energy, then jogging is the proper choice. Keeping her mind fixed on those goals will help her to see that she is making progress despite ending up in the same location where she started.

If our goals in practicing the spiritual disciplines are immediate results, sweeping feelings, and drastic change, we will quickly become discouraged. But these are not the purposes of the disciplines. They are meant to change us from the inside out—changing our brains, renewing our minds, and transforming our lives. Rob Moll describes this process: "Our behaviors and our actions can change the nature of our brain, which can change the content of our thoughts. At the

---

9. Owen, *Spiritual-Mindedness*, 199.
10. This list is from Donald Whitney, *Spiritual Disciplines for the Christian Life* (Colorado Springs, Colo.: NavPress, 2014), contents page.

same time, our very thoughts can cause the neurons in our brain to grow and change."[11] He goes on to say, "Here in the mundane routines of our day, the spiritual disciplines can quietly begin to reshape our minds as they introduce new patterns into our behavior…. We can be assured that our brains are reforming as our practices help to mold us more into the image of Jesus."[12]

Becoming more like Jesus is a process that takes time—a lifetime. This should not discourage us but encourage us to build godly, disciplined habits now because we know God will work through them over time. Seventeenth-century Puritan George Swinnock instructs, "Neglect not private or public ordinances. Your bodies may as probably live without diet, as your souls without duties. This is God's way, by which He infuseth grace where it is wanting, and increaseth grace where it is."[13] Habitually practicing the spiritual disciplines is the Spirit's ordinary way of leading us to grow fruit.[14] It is not our actions that produce fruit but God's power working in and through our obedience. Richard Foster writes:

> A farmer is helpless to grow grain; all he can do is provide the right conditions for the growing of grain…. The Disciplines are God's way of getting us into the ground; they put us where he can work within us and transform us. By themselves the Spiritual Disciplines can do nothing; they can only get us to the place where something can be done.[15]

God is the one who does all the work of renewing our minds and transforming our lives. At the same time, He tells us what we should be saying and doing. This is hard for us to understand, but if we trust

---

11. Moll, *What Your Body Knows about God*, 22.

12. Moll, *What Your Body Knows about God*, 124–25.

13. As quoted in I. D. E. Thomas, comp., *The Golden Treasury of Puritan Quotations* (Chicago: Moody Press, 1975), 181.

14. Maarten Kuivenhoven, "Christ Cares for His Church" (sermon, Heritage Reformed Congregation, Grand Rapids, Mich., February 9, 2020), https://www.sermonaudio.com/sermoninfo.asp?SID=21420229203416.

15. Richard Foster, *Celebration of Discipline: The Path to Spiritual Growth* (New York: HarperCollins, 1998), 7.

Him, then we will do as He instructs despite our lack of full understanding. We will speak and act according to His word, knowing that He will renew our minds as we obey. And we will think according to His word, knowing that He will transform our lives as we obey. Let's look at some specific examples of truths to think about and how these truths transform our words and actions.

Think about Who God Is

In high school I had a friend who disliked chemistry because of how it was taught. The teacher would have the students learn how to work through an equation first and later explained why the equation was necessary. My friend thought she would learn better if she knew why the equation was necessary before she had to work through it. But the teacher knew best. He knew that without learning the equation first, it would be impossible for the students to understand the "why." They had to recognize their teacher's wisdom and trust him enough to be willing to learn the equation before they understood why it was useful.

The same is true for us and God. We must recognize His wisdom and goodness and trust Him enough to be willing to obey Him no matter what, even though we do not yet understand why He requires certain things of us. Proverbs 3:5–6 says,

> Trust in the LORD with all your heart,
> And lean not on your own understanding;
> In all your ways acknowledge Him,
> And He shall direct your paths.

Throughout the Bible, we see examples of this need to trust God rather than our own understanding. In a seventeenth-century sermon, Thomas Manton shows how even when we cannot see the connection between what God tells us to do and the result we are hoping for—such as when God told Naaman to wash in the Jordan River so that he would be healed—we must still take God's way.[16] This type of trust requires thinking about and meditating on who God is. When

---

16. Thomas Manton, *Eighteen Sermons on the Second Chapter of the Second*

we spend time thinking about how good and merciful God is and how much greater and wiser He is than we are, we begin to realize that it makes no sense to speak and act in a way that contradicts Scripture. He is our Creator, after all! He knows how we work best, and the Bible is His way of sharing that information with us.

Thinking about who God is also leads us to think about who we are. We begin to realize more and more how limited we are in our thinking and how we cannot possibly understand all the reasons He has for the commands He gives. But our lack of understanding should not keep us from obeying God. It should actually encourage us to obey Him because we know there is more to the story than we can see now. The amazing result of speaking and acting in obedience by the power of the Holy Spirit is that He renews our minds, giving us greater insight and making us more and more willing to obey Him. So don't wait for full understanding before you begin to obey God. Instead, trust Him, think about who He is, and speak and act accordingly.

One example of how thinking about who God is changes what we say and do is prayer. We know that God wants us to pray to Him, but we don't fully understand how prayer works. If we are not thinking about who God is, then we will rely on our own logic. When prayer doesn't seem to have an immediate effect in our lives, we stop praying. But when we do think about who God is, we remember that His knowledge is infinitely greater than ours, and so we trust that He knows best. Because He knows best and tells us to pray, we pray. Our thinking influences us to pray, and then the act of praying influences our thoughts. Rob Moll writes, "In spiritual practices, the attention required in deep prayer and contemplation, study or worship is what the brain needs to grow and enhance neural connections."[17] Our brains are physically changed as we pray to God, but more importantly, our faith in God is strengthened and our dependence on Him

---

Epistle to the Thessalonians, in *The Complete Works of Thomas Manton* (London: James Nisbet, 1871), 3:124.

17. Moll, *What Your Body Knows about God*, 163.

is deepened. Think about who God is, and allow that thinking to encourage you in your prayer life.

Think about Who You Are in Christ

In today's world, there is a lot of emphasis on identity. People try to figure out at all costs who they really are. And there is something to be said about knowing who you are. How you think of yourself changes what you say and do. James Clear remarks, "When you have repeated a story to yourself for years, it is easy to slide into these mental grooves and accept them as a fact. In time, you begin to resist certain actions because 'that's not who I am.'"[18] As Christians, we don't have to go on a desperate search to try to figure out what story to tell ourselves or what our identity is. If we are in Christ, our true identity is presented to us in the Bible. John Rinehart gives these examples (and many others): "You are now a saint, a servant, a steward, and a soldier (Romans 1:7; Acts 26:16; 1 Peter 4:10; 2 Timothy 2:3). You are a witness and a worker (Acts 1:8; Ephesians 2:10). Through Jesus you are victorious (1 Corinthians 15:57). You have a glorious future (Romans 8:18). You are a citizen of heaven (Philippians 3:20). You are an ambassador for my Son (2 Corinthians 5:20)."[19]

We must spend time actively thinking about our new identity because doing so offers motivation and energy to live according to it. In Romans 6:11 Paul writes, "Likewise you also, *reckon* yourselves to be dead indeed to sin, but alive to God in Christ Jesus our Lord." The word translated here as "reckon" can also be translated as "count," "consider," or "think of." As we are thinking of ourselves as dead to sin and alive to God in Christ, Paul instructs,

---

18. James Clear, *Atomic Habits: An Easy and Proven Way to Build Good Habits and Break Bad Ones* (New York: Avery, 2018), 35. To learn more about the Christian's true identity in Christ, see Jonathan Landry Cruse, *The Christian's True Identity: What It Means to Be in Christ* (Grand Rapids: Reformation Heritage Books, 2019).

19. John Rinehart, "What God Thinks about You," Articles, Desiring God, September 24, 2015, https://www.desiringgod.org/articles/what-god-thinks-about-you.

Therefore do not let sin reign in your mortal body, that you should obey it in its lusts. And do not present your members as instruments of unrighteousness to sin, but present yourselves to God as being alive from the dead, and your members as instruments of righteousness to God. For sin shall not have dominion over you, for you are not under law but under grace. (Rom. 6:12–14)

Did you notice the word "therefore"? With this word Paul connects our identity with what we do. The reason he gives for not letting sin reign is who we are: we are dead to sin and alive to God. And the way we connect these two things in real life is by thinking about who we are. Without thinking about how we are dead to sin and alive to God, we will continue to let sin reign, to obey our lusts, and to present our bodies as instruments of unrighteousness. But if we consider who we are in Christ—if we get into the mental groove of repeating to ourselves, *This action no longer aligns with my identity in Christ. I have put off the old man with his deeds, and I have put on the new man* (Col. 3:9–10). *I will not present my body as an instrument of unrighteousness to sin but of righteousness to God* (Rom. 6:12–14)—then, by the power of the Holy Spirit, sin will not have dominion over us.

Here are some examples. When faced with the temptation to speak critically of someone, we think, *That's not who I am. In Christ, I am dead to sin and alive to God. I speak in love.* When deciding whether to indulge in sexual sin, we think, *That's not who I am. In Christ, I have put off the old man and have put on the new. I do not live according to the flesh.* When feeling the urge to lash out in impatience, we think, *That's not who I am. In Christ, I am no longer a slave to sin. I am under grace and act graciously.* These ways of thinking about who we are in Christ according to Scripture should stop us in our tracks by the power of the Holy Spirit and keep us from speaking or acting in sin. And when we do speak and act according to our true identity in Christ, it is reinforced in our minds that that is who we are. Though we may not win every individual battle, we know that we will win the war because who we are changes what we say and do. "I have been crucified with Christ; it is no longer I who live, but Christ lives in me; and the life which I now live in the flesh I live by faith in the Son of God, who loved me and gave Himself for me" (Gal. 2:20).

Think about What God's Will for You Is

Another truth that we must spend time thinking about is that God's will for us is sanctification (1 Thess. 4:3). When my friends and I were younger, we were very concerned about what God's will for us was. What jobs should we apply for? Where should we go to college? Would we get married and, if so, to whom? These were the questions that weighed on our minds when we thought about God's will. While it was good for us to pray about these questions and turn to God as we sought answers, we were missing the essence of what the Bible teaches about what God's will is for us—sanctification.

Living according to God's will for us is not just about making these big life decisions but about taking every opportunity for obedience by walking in the Spirit (Gal. 5:25). The Bible is not filled with verses that give us the right choice for every major life decision. It *is* filled with verses about how we are to think, speak, and act throughout all of life, no matter what decisions must be made or what our circumstances are. We never need to question whether God wants us to react to a situation in hate or love, self-indulgence or self-control, pride or humility.

When we are thinking in this way, we become less obsessed with the big decisions of our lives and more concerned with the little ones. After all, what feels little to us is actually very important to God. It's the little decisions that determine whether we are making progress in sanctification or not. And what feels big to us is often not even a choice between a sinful option or a holy option but simply a choice among several good options. The big things are important and require great wisdom, but it's the little things in daily life that determine who we are becoming.

For example, we can accept the right job, attend the right college, and marry the right spouse but still live in a way that is not according to God's will. Are we working with integrity in our job, being honest with and kind to customers and managers? Are we witnessing to the students and professors at our college, with both the way we live and the words we say? Are we serving and loving our spouses in big and small ways—when they are deserving and when they are not? These little daily choices will tell us more about how sanctified we are than the major life decisions. And when we are habitually living according to God's will in small daily deeds, our minds are being trained to always think according to what He would have us do. This renews our minds and increases our discernment, giving us more clarity when the major decisions do come up. Spending time thinking about this truth will help us to recognize the importance of every little decision and to live in obedience to God regardless of whether the decision in front of us feels big or little.

Think about How God Makes You Like Jesus

We should also think about why God wants us to live according to His word in daily life, whether we are facing big or small decisions about what to say and do. He is not an arbitrary God, throwing out commands here and there just to see if we will obey Him. He wants what is best for us, and what is best for us is that we be conformed to the image of Jesus, no matter what it takes. In Romans 8:28, we read, "And we know that all things work together for good to those who love God, to those who are the called according to His purpose." We tend to quote this verse as if it means only that the events and circumstances in our lives will somehow lead to better, more "desirable" events and circumstances in a few months or a few years. But this is a very earthly view. We forget about the next verse, which completes the thought: "For whom He foreknew, He also predestined to be conformed to the image of His Son, that He might be the firstborn among many brethren" (v. 29). What is good for us is not that everything "works out" in this life but that we are conformed to the image of Jesus. And how does God conform us to the image of Jesus? He renews our minds and transforms our lives as we live in obedience in all that we think, say, and do.

> So now present your members as slaves to righteousness *leading to* sanctification. (Rom. 6:19 ESV)

> You have purified your souls *in obeying* the truth through the Spirit in sincere love of the brethren. (1 Peter 1:22)

> And the LORD commanded us to observe all these statutes, to fear the LORD our God, *for our good always*, that He might preserve us alive, as it is this day. Then it will be righteousness for us, if we are careful to observe all these commandments before the LORD our God, as He has commanded us. (Deut. 6:24–25)

We do not work this obedience in our own hearts, and we certainly do not sanctify ourselves. But still, we obey when we feel like obeying and when we don't, and God works through our obedience, just as He worked through the steps of the Israelites who walked around Jericho to do a work that was far greater than the mere act of walking could have done on its own. Each moment that we walk by the Spirit is a moment we are not setting our minds on the things of the flesh (Rom. 8:5) or gratifying the desires of the flesh (Gal. 5:16). And each moment that we choose to live according to the Spirit and not the flesh is a moment that leads to godly fruit, to sanctification, to Christlikeness, to life.

Think about this over and over so that it becomes ingrained in your decision-making process. Every decision we make, big or small, is a choice between gratifying the flesh or walking by the Spirit. Every step we take in gratifying the flesh is a step toward becoming less like Jesus, and every step we take according to the Spirit is a step toward becoming more like Him. Which is your goal? To become less like Him, or to become more like Him? If your goal is to become more like Him, is what you are about to say or do going to bring you closer to that goal? If not, is it really worth it?

Examples of how this plays out in real life come up every day, whenever we are given an opportunity to serve someone else. We know that Jesus spent His life on earth serving others. He told His disciples, "I am among you as the One who serves" (Luke 22:27), and His life was evidence that this was true. Whenever we are given an opportunity to serve, whether by picking up our family's dirty socks or passing along a drive-through meal to a homeless person, our decision of what to do and our attitude while we do it provides evidence of what we are thinking. If we are not thinking about being like Christ, we will grumble as we do the necessary housework and avert our eyes as we pass by someone in need. But if we are regularly thinking about being like Christ, we can serve others with joy. Jesus, the King of kings, washed the feet of His disciples. Can we not wash the clothing of our family with joy? Jesus, the Lord of lords, gave up His life to save us. Can we not give up a meal to encourage a hungry person? Christ's entire mindset was centered on serving others. As we learn to speak and act in service to others, by the power of the Holy Spirit our mindsets too will shift to become more service oriented. In other words, we will more and more have the mind of Christ.

Think about the Reward of Obedience

Another truth that is crucial to think about is that God wants what is good for His children. His desire for our good is part of why He wants us to live in obedience to Him. Obedience is good for us not just because it conforms us to the image of Jesus but also because it leads to life and disobedience leads to death. Every command and instruction in the Bible is given to teach us how to walk in God's ways, and He longs for us to walk in His ways because they lead to holiness, the way of life.

> Behold, I set before you today a blessing and a curse: the blessing, if you obey the commandments of the LORD your God which I command you today; and the curse, if you do not obey the commandments of the LORD your God, but turn aside from the way which I command you today, to go after other gods which you have not known. (Deut. 11:26–28)

> "As I live," says the Lord GOD, "I have no pleasure in the death of the wicked, but that the wicked turn from his way and live. Turn, turn from your evil ways! For why should you die, O house of Israel?" (Ezek. 33:11)

He who keeps the commandment keeps his soul, but he who is careless of his ways will die. (Prov. 19:16)

Do you not know that to whom you present yourselves slaves to obey, you are that one's slaves whom you obey, whether of sin leading to death, or of obedience leading to righteousness?… I speak in human terms because of the weakness of your flesh. For just as you presented your members as slaves of uncleanness, and of lawlessness leading to more lawlessness, so now present your members as slaves of righteousness for holiness….

But now having been set free from sin, and having become slaves of God, you have your fruit to holiness, and the end, everlasting life. For the wages of sin is death, but the gift of God is eternal life in Christ Jesus our Lord. (Rom. 6:16, 19, 22–23)

For if you live according to the flesh you will die; but if by the Spirit you put to death the deeds of the body, you will live. (Rom. 8:13)

Do we really believe these verses? Or do we prove by our words and actions that we do not take them seriously? When what we say and do contradicts the Bible, there is often some pleasure associated with the sin, but it is so fleeting. When we speak and act according to Scripture, there is often some self-denial associated with the holy action, but the rewards are so great! David Guzik writes, "Doing good is often difficult because as a general rule, evil is rewarded immediately and the reward of doing good is often delayed. But the rewards of good are better and far more secure than the rewards of doing evil."[20] We must spend less time thinking about what might feel good in the moment and more time thinking about the rewards that God Himself promises for doing good.

Changing the focus of our thoughts in this way will have influence over how we speak and act. Think of the countless promises God has given us that connect obedience with a specific reward. He follows this pattern over and over again: "If you do this, I will give you that." "Ask,

20. David Guzik, Enduring Word Bible Commentary (website), on 1 Peter 3:11, accessed February 10, 2021, https://enduringword.com/bible-commentary/1-peter-3/.

and it will be given to you; seek, and you will find; knock, and it will be opened to you" (Matt. 7:7). It is good for us to think about the rewards of obedience. Nineteenth-century theologian Charles Hodge explains that "it is right to present to men the divinely ordained consequences of their actions as motives to control their conduct. It is right to tell men that obedience to God, devotion to His glory and the good of others, will effectually promote their own welfare."[21]

When we trust God enough to believe that His promises of rewards are true, and when we focus more on the reward for the action than on whether we feel like doing the action in the moment, then we are on our way to speaking and acting in obedience to His word. For example, we might feel like pushing the snooze button on our alarm, but we know that God rewards those who diligently seek Him, and so we get out of bed to pray and study the Bible. Or we might feel like watching something that our conscience tells us we shouldn't, but we know that it will only lead us into sin, and so we choose to do something else with our time. It takes faith to choose the reward at the end of the path over the pleasure at the beginning, but the more we think about the reward, the easier holy choices become.

Obeying God is an often mundane, sometimes agonizing, yet gloriously rewarded journey that requires a change in who we are at the very core of our being. God also uses our obedience to create change in us and transform us into the image of His only begotten Son! We obey not because of who we are or how we feel in this moment but because of who God is and what He promises as the end result of obedience. "Moreover by [the judgments of the Lord] Your servant is warned, and in keeping them there is great reward" (Ps. 19:11).

Think about the Effort Required for Obedience

When attempting to speak and act in obedience to the commandments of God, we often forget to consider the truth that obedience

---

21. As quoted by Mike Riccardi, "Freely and Cheerfully: Part 1" (conference address, PRTS Conference 2020, Grand Rapids, Mich., August 27, 2020), https://www.sermonaudio.com/sermoninfo.asp?SID=8262018355120.

requires effort. It is not something that feels natural or happens automatically for the Christian. Seventeenth-century Scottish pastor Samuel Rutherford writes,

> It cost Christ and all His followers sharp showers and hot sweats ere they won to the top of the mountain. But still our soft nature would have heaven coming to our bedside when we are sleeping, and lying down with us, that we might go to heaven in warm clothes; but all that came there found wet feet by the way, and sharp storms that did take the hide off their face, and found tos and fros, and ups and downs, and many enemies by the way.[22]

Think of the language the Bible so often uses when it is talking about obedience. It is the language of work, exercise, and battle. We are instructed to walk (Gal. 5:16, 25), sow (6:8), work out (Phil. 2:12–13), and practice (4:9 ESV). Paul thanks God for the Thessalonians' "work of faith" and "labor of love" (1 Thess. 1:3). The word "labor" used here implies intense labor united with trouble and toil.[23] Elsewhere, Paul instructs Timothy, "Exercise yourself toward godliness" (1 Tim. 4:7), and "Give yourself entirely to" these things and "continue in them" (vv. 15–16). He also tells Timothy, "I have fought the good fight, I have finished the race, I have kept the faith" (2 Tim. 4:7). The author of Hebrews encourages his audience, "Let us run with endurance the race that is set before us" (Heb. 12:1). Jesus Himself speaks of taking up the cross and following Him (Matt. 16:24). These verses reveal the difficulty of obedience and the great amount of effort required for it.

But this should not discourage us! This effort that is asked of us is not what saves us but is the result of our salvation. Jesus Christ completing the work of salvation on the cross once and for all is what gives us energy for the effort of obedience. If anything, that obedience requires effort should encourage us, because who among

---

22. Samuel Rutherford, *Letters of the Rev. Samuel Rutherford* (New York: Robert Carter and Brothers, 1875), 298, https://www.google.com/books/edition /Letters_of_the_Rev_Samuel_Rutherford_wit/dEdQAQAAMAAJ?hl=en&gbpv=1.

23. *Strong's Lexicon*, s.v., "kopos," accessed March 17, 2021, https://www .blueletterbible.org/lang/lexicon/lexicon.cfm?t=kjv&strongs=g2873.

us feels that obedience to God's word comes easily and naturally on a regular basis? If obedience were automatic in the Christian's life, if it were something that just happened to us, the Bible would not need to include so much instruction about how to live the Christian life. But it does. Over and over the Bible provides us with knowledge about God and then proceeds to tell us how we are to live now that we have this knowledge. It tells us how to think and then what to say and do in response to that thinking.

God has provided us not only with knowledge through Scripture but also with power by His Spirit to enable us to obey. In Ezekiel 36:27, God tells the Israelites, "I will put My Spirit within you and cause you to walk in My statutes, and you will keep My judgments and do them." We too desperately need God to work in us so that we can obey from the heart, and we must pray that He will. I'm afraid too many of us are waiting for some sort of magical turbo boost of power before we obey. We are putting off the effort because we think that Holy Spirit power should make obedience feel easy. We forget that we live in a fallen world and are still in the flesh with a battle going on between our old and new natures. Until we arrive in heaven, obedience will not be easy. While we run the race set before us, the power of the Holy Spirit is less like the runner's high that makes running easy and more like the muscle that makes running possible.

Maybe you are a nurse trying to care for an ungrateful patient, a teacher trying to help a stubborn student, or a parent trying to train up a disobedient child in the way that he should go. Speaking and acting in obedience to God's word is difficult in these and countless other situations. Our flesh calls for us to lash out in anger, impatience, or frustration. It takes immense effort to hold back and to instead speak and act with love, patience, and gentleness. This is because we are not yet totally transformed. But the effort it takes to obey will be worth it, and the power of Him who raised Jesus Christ from the dead is within us to help us in our efforts. Think about this truth often. Remember the effort required for obedience and the power that enables you to obey, and then persevere, no matter how unsteady your efforts are.

Think about the Learning and Strategy Required for Obedience

Not only do we forget that obedience requires effort but also that it requires learning and strategy. When my first baby was born, I remember being surprised that so much of motherhood did not feel natural or automatic to me. Somehow I had expected that giving birth to a baby would instantly give me a new set of skills, even though I had not practiced those skills before. Many Christians have the same expectation about living the Christian life. We subconsciously think that because we have believed on the Lord Jesus Christ, we will instantly gain the ability to speak and act the way a Christian should. And when obedience doesn't come automatically, we are disappointed in ourselves and may even question whether we truly believed in the first place.

But Jesus did not expect this of His disciples, and He does not expect it of us. Think of how He taught His disciples. He lived with them for three years, showing them by His daily example what it looked like to speak and act in a way that is fitting for one who believes in God. Yet even after three years with Jesus, they were not perfected. They still had much to learn and work on, and we do too. Speaking and acting like Jesus isn't something that just happens spontaneously. E. Randolph Richards and Brandon J. O'Brien explain that in our Western culture, we place more value on the virtuous acts that are spontaneous rather than the ones that are a result of discipline and habit. But this is not the case in Scripture: "As it is described in Scripture, developing virtue is a process that begins with our thoughts and results in our deeds…. It almost sounds self-righteous to Westerners. But what the psalmist is describing is a determination to pursue godliness."[24]

This idea of pursuing godliness might make us uncomfortable because we feel it strays into the camp of self-help literature, and we

---

24. E. Randolph Richards and Brandon J. O'Brien, *Misreading Scripture with Western Eyes: Removing Cultural Blinders to Better Understand the Bible* (Downers Grove, Ill.: InterVarsity, 2012), 182–83.

know that we need the Spirit's help. But just because the Spirit helps us does not mean we sit back and do nothing. We must be like David, who resolved to "behave wisely in a perfect way" (Ps. 101:2); Ezra, who "prepared his heart to seek the Law of the LORD, and to do it" (Ezra 7:10); and Daniel, who "purposed in his heart that he would not defile himself" (Dan. 1:8). We must be learning about what the Christian life actually looks like from the examples of Jesus and others in the Bible and from the godly people in our communities. We must be strategizing and asking questions of others about how we can obey God more consistently. What sins are particularly tantalizing to us? How can we flee from temptation and resist the devil in those areas? What can we read or listen to that will encourage us toward righteous living? Is there a more mature Christian God has placed in our lives whom we can talk to about this issue?

As we think in this way, we speak and act in response. Maybe we call a trusted member of our church community to confess a sin that we have been hiding in darkness for far too long. Maybe we take an elderly person out for coffee and ask her questions about how she has fought sin and served the Lord throughout her life. Maybe we install an internet filter that makes it impossible for us to access specific sites. Maybe we take up running because we know that we tend to struggle less with impatience when we have exercised. We are fighting against principalities and powers, and yet our fight often comes down to simple strategic daily habits and decisions. John Owen states,

> We need to be intimately acquainted with the ways, wiles, methods, advantages, and occasions which give lust its success. This is how men deal with their enemies. They search out their plans, ponder their goals, and consider how and by what means they have prevailed over them in the past. Then they can be defeated. Without this kind of strategic thinking, warfare is very primitive. Those who indeed mortify lust deal with it in this way.[25]

---

25. Owen, *Mortification of Sin*, 37.

We depend on God's Spirit, not our strategy, but the power of the Spirit does not negate the benefits of learning strategic obedience to God's word. Like the psalmist in Psalm 119:59, we think about our ways, and if they do not match up with the ways of God, we turn our feet to walk in obedience to God's commands.

Think about How Suffering Leads to Glory

Another way that God shapes our thinking and makes us more like Jesus is through trials. Every trial that we go through changes us. Either it draws us closer to God, helping us trust Him more, or it pushes us away from God, making us more cynical and bitter. The difference is in how we think about our trials.

As always, the Bible instructs us in how we should think. In Romans 5:3–4, we read, "We also glory in tribulations, *knowing* that tribulation produces perseverance; and perseverance, character; and character, hope." When Paul uses lists like these, it can be helpful to draw them out with arrows: tribulation → perseverance → character → hope. What does this list teach us? We will go through trials. But if we are saved by the grace of God and turn to Him in our trials, He will use them to grow perseverance, character, and hope in our lives. A. Craig Troxel confirms, "Godly character comes by trial. Difficulties strain us and reveal whether our knowledge of Christ has sunk down into our spiritual bones."[26] This is how we can glory in our trials instead of despairing: we *know* what they can produce in the life of the Christian.

But knowing this takes faith and hope, which don't come naturally to the sinful mind. Our minds are so set on the world and the desires of our flesh that we tend to think more about our current comforts than about our future character. This is why trials are so hard for us, and this is why they are so good for us. Without trials, we would be so content with the deceitful comforts of this world, so stuffed full with what it offers, that we would never turn to God. We would never be hungry for something more. When we are stripped

---

26. Troxel, *With All Your Heart*, 138.

of our comforts, something changes in our minds. We have to find something else to think about, someone else to turn to. If God is who we turn to, the pathways in our brains that turn to Him in need are strengthened and the paths that turn to other things are weakened. This is a true blessing. So often we thank God for the blessings of food and clothing and health and wealth, but we forget to thank Him for the far greater blessings of whatever He has put into our lives to turn us to Him and make us more like Jesus. Can we not give up some of our temporary comforts in exchange for what God can work in our lives? Second Corinthians 4:17–18 declares, "Our light affliction, which is but for a moment, is working for us a far more exceeding and eternal weight of glory, while we do not look at the things which are seen, but at the things which are not seen. For the things which are seen are temporary, but the things which are not seen are eternal."

It is not just that glory comes after suffering. It is that somehow affliction and suffering are what God uses in our lives to work that glory for us. Crossing a finish line means nothing to the person who did not run the race. But to those who run, crossing it is everything. It is what motivates them to keep running despite pain and difficulty, and it is what rewards them when they finish the race. Running the race is what gives meaning to that line across the road, and suffering is part of what gives meaning to glory.

When we by faith think in this future-focused way, knowing that eternal glory is our motivation and reward, then what we say and do changes. Instead of complaining and despairing when trials come, we praise God and live in a way that honors Him. We keep saying our prayers, going to church, and singing in worship—not because we always feel like it but because we know the end of the story, and we know that it will be good and glorious. And as we continue to speak and act according to this knowledge, our minds are renewed and our lives transformed. Eugene Peterson describes two types of people: "One person says, 'I don't feel like worshiping; therefore I am not going to church. I will wait till I feel like it and then I will go.' Another says, 'I don't feel like worshiping; therefore I will go to church and put myself in the way of worship.' In the process she finds herself blessed and begins, in turn, to bless."[27]

Knowing what suffering produces in our lives and knowing that it works glory for us means that we don't collapse at the side of the road on our way to heaven; rather, we continue to worship God. We know what is coming, and so we run or walk or crawl our race with endurance. And one day, when we cross that finish line into heaven, we will do nothing but rejoice. Seeing Jesus and experiencing glory will make suffering all worth it.

But we have not reached heaven yet. While we are still in this world, we must live in obedience to God in all that we think and in all that we say and do, knowing that they influence each other, knowing that obedience in our thought life will encourage obedience in our words and actions, and vice versa. So *think* according to His word. Think about who God is and who you are in Christ. Think about what God's will for you is, how He is working to make you more like Jesus, and what is truly good for you. Think about the effort, learning, and strategy that are required for obedience. Think about how suffering leads to glory. As God renews your mind through the knowledge He has given, what you *say* and *do* will be transformed to more and more reflect this proper, holy, biblical, Christlike thinking.

---

27. Eugene H. Peterson, *A Long Obedience in the Same Direction: Discipleship in an Instant Society* (Downers Grove, Ill.: InterVarsity, 2000), 195.

5

FEEL AND DESIRE

Follow your heart! Do what feels best! Don't let anyone tell you what's right for you! The world bombards us with messages like these. The stories it tells in books and movies lead us to believe that our feelings are true and trustworthy and that we can and should act on whatever it is that we are feeling. The solutions it offers in articles and podcasts imply that what feels best must be what is best for us. But the Bible shares a different message. Jeremiah 17:9 describes our hearts as "deceitful above all things" and "desperately wicked." James 1:14–15 says, "Each one is tempted when he is drawn away by his own desires and enticed. Then, when desire has conceived, it gives birth to sin; and sin, when it is full-grown, brings forth death." Do we really want to base our life on what our naturally deceitful, desperately wicked hearts feel and desire?

Common sense lines up with the Bible. What feels best in the moment in our daily lives almost always leads to a less-desired outcome in the future. We procrastinate on work because we want to relax but then feel stressed the next day when we need to do twice as much work. We eat more than we need because the food tastes so good but then feel lethargic and too full. What feels good now will feel bad later. Elisabeth Elliot writes, "The modern mind easily confuses emotions and facts. If it feels good, do it! What is good, it is generally assumed, ought to make us feel good. For example, if it is the will of God, we will feel good about it. This is not always the case. Jonah had no good feelings about going to Nineveh. He preferred Joppa and started in that direction, to his own sorrow and that of his shipmates."[1]

When we choose to follow our heart, we base our decisions about what to look at and listen to on what we feel like consuming, which has immense influence over what we think and therefore over what we say and do. Our thoughts, words, and actions then work together, influencing how we feel and what we desire. As Sinclair Ferguson says, "Our feelings and emotions are not isolated from our thinking and willing but guided by them."[2]

So what it comes down to is this: Will we follow the example of the world and base our lives—everything we consume, think, say, and do—on what we feel and desire at any given moment? Or will we base our lives on Scripture despite what we might be feeling or desiring? As R. C. Sproul points out, "Our calling isn't to follow our hearts. Our calling is to have our hearts informed and directed by the clear and plain teaching of the Word of God." There are times that our feelings and desires will line up with God's word, and in those times we can follow our hearts because that is when we, like David, are people "after God's own heart." But in the life of every Christian, there are also many times that our feelings and desires do not line up with God's word. Paul struggled with this when he said, "For what I am doing, I do not understand. For what I will to do, that I do not practice; but what I hate, that I do" (Rom. 7:15). It is in these times that the spiritual battle becomes real and we must make a choice. In all that we look at, listen to, think, say, and do, will we follow our hearts or will we follow God's word?

What You Look at and Listen to Influences Your Feelings and Desires

How can we follow God's word when it goes against everything we are feeling or desiring in a particular moment? We can begin by examining what we are looking at and listening to on a regular basis.

---

1. Elliot, *Joyful Surrender*, 137.
2. Ferguson, *Let's Study Philippians*, 102.

When our physical bodies don't feel well, we might think about what we have eaten recently that could be making us sick. And when our minds and hearts are not "feeling well," when our feelings and desires do not line up with God's word, we should examine what we have been consuming mentally. If we have been consuming too much mental junk food—too much or the wrong kind of social media, news, movies, or TV shows—and if we have not been spending much time reading and hearing Scripture, is it any wonder our feelings and desires are not doing well? Eighteenth-century American theologian Jonathan Edwards points out, "Holy affections are not heat without light; but evermore arise from the information of the understanding, some spiritual instruction that the mind receives, some light or actual knowledge."[3]

When we choose what to consistently watch or read or listen to, we are choosing our future feelings and desires. To most often choose the knowledge of the world over the knowledge of God is to choose to turn our feelings and desires away from how God created us. As Jen Wilkin explains, "The heart cannot love what the mind does not know."[4]

Yet even when we are consuming the proper mental nutrition, our feelings and desires are not always trustworthy. This is because we are living with bodies and minds that have been broken by sin. Even simple physical needs like hunger or lack of sleep can totally change what we are feeling. We must have a source on which to rely that is more trustworthy than our own bodies and minds. That source is God and the Bible. John Piper emphasizes this:

> My feelings are not God. God is God. My feelings do not define truth. God's word defines truth. My feelings are echoes and responses to what my mind perceives. And sometimes—many times—my feelings are out of sync with the truth. When that happens—and it happens every day in some measure—I try not

---

3. Jonathan Edwards, *The Religious Affections* (1746; repr., Mineola, N.Y.: Dover, 2013), 192.

4. Wilkin, *Women of the Word*, 31.

to bend the truth to justify my imperfect feelings, but rather, I plead with God: Purify my perception of your truth and transform my feelings so that they are in sync with the truth.[5]

As Piper explains, transformation of our feelings and desires depends on right perception of God and His word, and that takes time, study, and prayer. Our minds will not be renewed without God's word. This does not mean that spending time in the Bible will make the change in our feelings and desires instant or consistent, but it will make a difference over time. Geoffrey Thomas states, "Let the Word break over your heart and mind again and again as the years go by, and imperceptibly there will come great changes in your attitude and outlook and conduct."[6] That is what God promises—His word will not return to Him void (Isa. 55:11). Rob Moll comments, "Prayer, meditation on Scripture and all other spiritual disciplines are not simply reminders like strings tied to our fingers. Instead, they shape our emotions. The disciplines teach and enable us to live by deeper truths and in accord with a deeper reality than the basic cravings of our bodies."[7] He further notes, "We often assume that feelings of devotions must inspire our daily prayer or devotional time. If we pray and don't 'feel' that God showed up, it's hard to keep going. But what if we could grow more and more like Christ, knowing that our daily faithful habits were building that relationship piece by piece? The knowledge of how our bodies are designed could provide the inspiration to keep trying, even when the work seems arduous."[8]

And so when we *feel* a lack of hope, faith, or love, we still turn our eyes and ears to Scripture because we trust that God will work through it over time to renew our minds and transform our lives, including our feelings and desires. We trust that the words of Psalm 19:7–11 are true:

5. John Piper, *Finally Alive: What Happens When We Are Born Again* (Rossshire, Scotland: Christian Focus, 2009), 165–66.

6. Geoffrey Thomas, *Reading the Bible* (Edinburgh: Banner of Truth, 1980), 22.

7. Moll, *What Your Body Knows about God*, 120.

8. Moll, *What Your Body Knows about God*, 166.

The law of the LORD is perfect, *converting* the soul;
The testimony of the LORD is sure, *making wise* the simple;
The statutes of the LORD are right, *rejoicing* the heart;
The commandment of the LORD is pure, *enlightening* the eyes;
The fear of the LORD is clean, *enduring* forever;
The judgments of the Lord are true and righteous altogether.
More to be desired are they than gold,
Yea, than much fine gold;
Sweeter also than honey and the honeycomb.
Moreover by them Your servant is warned,
And in keeping them there is great reward.

What You Think Influences Your Feelings and Desires

What we look at and listen to are not the only influences on our feelings and desires. What we think also has a lot of impact. English Puritan Thomas Goodwin writes, "Indeed, thoughts and affections are…the mutual causes of each other: 'Whilst I mused, the fire burned' (Psalm 39:3); so that thoughts are the bellows that kindle and inflame affections; and then if they are inflamed, they cause thoughts to boil."[9] When we intentionally think according to God's word in the ways we have already discussed in previous chapters, our feelings and desires can be flipped upside down. We don't think in obedience to the word of God because our feelings and desires have already been changed. We think in obedience because God asks it of us, and as we obey, He changes our feelings and desires. Changed thoughts produce changed feelings and desires. J. I. Packer suggests, "Think against your feelings; argue yourself out of the gloom they have spread; unmask the belief they have nourished; take yourself in hand, talk to yourself, make yourself look up from your problems to the God of the gospel; let *evangelical* thinking correct *emotional* thinking."[10]

Correcting our feelings through thinking is part of maturing both as a human and as a Christian. For example, babies cry because

---

9. Thomas Goodwin, "The Vanity of Thoughts," in *The Works of Thomas Goodwin* (Eureka, Calif.: Tanski Publications, 1996), 3:526–27.

10. Packer, *Knowing God*, 259–60 (emphasis original).

they are hungry. To tell them that they will eat in five minutes has no effect on how much they cry because they cannot reason themselves out of those hungry feelings. But adults can reason with themselves that even though they are hungry, their meal will be ready soon and therefore they can wait for that meal without crying. As we mature in our Christian walk of life, we learn to use our thinking to determine our feelings rather than letting our feelings determine our thinking.

One example of this in the Christian life is the feeling of peace. We might pray to God, asking why we don't feel any peace, all the while ignoring what God tells us in the Bible about peace. Because we lack peace, we allow our thinking to be chaotic, to dwell on those very circumstances that are contributing to our lack of peace. But God tells us to use our thinking to determine our feelings, to think in a certain way in order to feel His peace. It is those whose minds are fixed on Him who will be kept in perfect peace (Isa. 26:3) and that peace will guard our hearts and minds when we are letting Him know our requests through prayer, supplication, and thanksgiving (Phil. 4:5–7). If we are not keeping our minds fixed on Him, thinking about how powerful and good and merciful and kind and all-knowing He is, and if we are not praying to Him and thanking Him—even giving thanks for the trial we are walking through right now—then how can we expect peace? We must think in the way He tells us to think in order to feel the peace that He promises.

Another example of this is how God combats fear in the lives of His people. When people in the Bible are told not to fear, they are often given the reason: God is with them. But if they are not thinking that God is with them, then the fear returns. When Peter was walking on water, he began to sink the moment that He looked away from Jesus. When we "look away" from Jesus in our minds, when we allow our feelings to take over and forget to think about how He is with us and is working all things together for our good, that is when we will begin to sink. Elisabeth Elliot points out, "Our feelings are very fleeting and ephemeral, aren't they? We can't depend on them for five minutes at a time. But dwelling on the love, faithfulness, and mercy of God is always safe."

When we are thinking about God and what He instructs us to think about, setting our minds on things above, bringing every thought into captivity, hiding God's word in our heart, remembering the deeds of the Lord, and looking at the things that are not seen—this is when our feelings and desires will align with Scripture. Do not underestimate the impact of every thought that passes through your mind.

What You Say and Do Influences Your Feelings and Desires

It is also important not to underestimate the impact of everything we say and do because our words and actions also have great influence over what we feel and desire. When we aren't paying attention, what we say and do is often guided by what we feel and desire. Because we feel like making a cutting remark, we do. Because we desire to commit a sinful action, we do. But a more godly way of living is to intentionally allow what we say and do to be guided by Scripture and the Holy Spirit. Then, when we are living in obedience to God's word by His power, our feelings and desires begin to align more with what God Himself feels and desires. Changed feelings and desires can be an outcome rather than a cause of our obedience.

In order to live this way, we must stretch our focus from short-term to long-term desires. This is true of everything good in our lives. Think of someone who hires a physical trainer. If the focus is on short-term desires for comfort and ease, then what the trainer is putting that person through makes no sense. The exercises are uncomfortable and painful and do not show immediate results. But if the focus is on long-term desires for strength and fitness, then the exercises make sense because the trainee trusts the trainer enough to know that these exercises are what will strengthen her body over time. Focus on the long-term desires of a stronger body means that muscle pain is not a source of regret but of encouragement—something is happening in the body that will benefit it and help achieve the long-term goal.

Christians too must choose between short-term and long-term desires many times each day. We live with both an old and a new nature, and we must acknowledge the battle that is going on between them. For every decision we make about what to say or do, we have two opposing desires within us. One desire is to satisfy the flesh—to say or do exactly what we feel like saying or doing in the moment. But this is the short-term desire. It will bring pleasure and satisfaction, but only for a moment. It will quickly lead to regret, guilt, and other negative results. The other desire is to walk by the Spirit—to say or do what we know is right and loving and in alignment with the Bible. This is the long-term desire. It may not be what we feel like doing in the moment, but it is what will bring the most glory to God and the most good in our lives. Rosaria Butterfield gives an example of this:

> While you may still have sinful desires, God equips you to not act on them. If you, by temperament and practice, have a problem with the sin of anger, God will give to you through his gift of sanctification (as you respond in love by applying yourself to the means of grace) the ability to control yourself. This does not mean that you will necessarily have a cessation of anger or angry feelings, but rather, you will have the ability to react differently as they emerge.[11]

Paul wrote to the Galatians of how to fight this battle against sinful feelings: "Walk in the Spirit, and you shall not fulfill the lust of the flesh" (Gal. 5:16). To gratify the flesh means we are choosing not to walk by the Spirit. To walk by the Spirit means we are choosing not to gratify the flesh. Which will we choose? If our focus is short-term, we'll choose the flesh because immediate pleasure is more desirable than hard effort. If our focus is long-term, we'll choose the Spirit because joy in the Lord is more desirable than the regret of sin. We must focus on the greater, long-term desire. We must crucify the flesh with its passions and desires by walking according to the Spirit because that is how the fruit of the Spirit is produced in our lives (Gal. 5:22–25).

---

11. Rosaria Butterfield, *Openness Unhindered* (Pittsburgh: Crown and Covenant, 2015), 53.

Short-Term Desire		Long-Term Desire
Pleasure	→	Regret
Effort	→	Joy

We know that our struggle between short-term and long-term desire, between living by the flesh and walking by the Spirit, will always be with us here on earth. But by the power of the Spirit, as we live in obedience to God's word over time, as our long-term desires become a stronger force in our lives, as we take step after step according to the Spirit and not according to the flesh, God does transform us. He does sanctify not only what we say and do but also what we feel and desire, helping us to feel more joy and peace in obedience, less desire to satisfy our own quest for comfort and ease, and more desire to honor and glorify Him.

Faith Is More than Feeling or Desire

In order to truly grasp how our feelings and desires are influenced by our minds and wills, we will use three examples—faith, hope, and love. When we think of faith, hope, and love, we might think of them as feelings. But these three basics of the Christian life do not involve just the emotions but also the mind and the will; they include Spirit-empowered choices to look, listen, think, speak, and act in faith-strengthening, hope-filling, love-overflowing, God-glorifying ways. When we do not feel like we are filled with faith, hope, or love, it may be a clue that how we are thinking and living is not aligning with God's word. Let's walk through each in order to correct our thinking of what it means to have faith, hope, and love.

When we think of faith, we might subconsciously assume that it is primarily made up of feelings. We hear others speak of their faith in Christ in exuberant terms, and when our emotions don't live up to theirs, we think that we must not have faith at all. But true faith in God is less about how we feel and more about who Christ is and what He has done. It is not by the strength of our emotions but by faith in Him given by Him that He saves us (Heb. 10:39), makes us

His children (John 1:12), gives us His righteousness (Phil. 3:9), and is bringing us to eternal life (John 6:40). Sixteenth-century clergyman Richard Greenham puts it simply: "Oh brother be of good comfort, we hold Christ by faith, and not by feeling."[12] So when we don't "feel" much faith, we turn to the Bible to see that although faith does change how we feel and what we desire, it encompasses so much more than feelings and desires.

First, what we look at and listen to influences our faith. The Bible tells us that "faith comes by hearing, and hearing by the word of God" (Rom. 10:17). It is through our hearing the word of God that God works faith in our hearts, and it is through continued hearing, searching, and looking to God for help that He strengthens our faith. Having faith in God means that we should strive for more time in the Bible, not less. And if we are going through a period in which we are feeling more doubt than faith, this should cause us to examine what we are looking at and listening to and spend even more time in the Bible. As Proverbs 22:17, 19 instructs,

> Incline your ear and hear the words of the wise,
> And apply your heart to my knowledge…
> So that your trust may be in the LORD;
> I have instructed you today, even you.

Second, what we think influences our faith. To spend time remembering how God has been faithful in the past strengthens our faith in Him for the future (Psalm 77). To spend time meditating on Scripture helps make us like a tree planted by rivers of water, yielding fruit in season (Psalm 1). This fruit includes the feelings of rootedness, confidence, and peace that result from faith-filled living. We cannot expect those feelings apart from thinking according to our faith.

Third, our faith influences what we say and do, and what we say and do influences the strength of our faith. Look over the list of

---

12. Richard Greenham, *Grave Counsels*, in Richard Greenham, Henry Holland, and Robert Hill, *The Workes of the Reverend…M. Richard Greenham…Collected into One Volume…* (London: printed [by Thomas Creede] for William Welby, 1612), 12. Spelling has been modernized.

people in the Hall of Faith chapter, Hebrews 11, and take note that the Bible uses verbs to show these believers' faith. "By faith Abel *offered*" (v. 4); "Enoch was *taken away*" (v. 5); "Noah...*moved*" and "*prepared*" (v. 7); Abraham "*went out*," "*dwelt*," "*waited*," and "*offered*" (vv. 8–9, 10, 17); "Sarah...*received* strength to conceive" (v. 11); "Isaac *blessed*"; "Jacob...*blessed*" (vv. 20–21); "Joseph...*made* mention...and *gave* instructions" (v. 22); "Moses...*was hidden*," "*refused*," "*choosing*," "*esteeming*," "*forsook*," "*endured*," "*kept*" (vv. 23, 25–28); the Israelites "*passed through*" (v. 29). This is language not of emotion but of action. We do not read whether Abraham felt like leaving Ur to go to an unknown place or whether Moses felt like choosing to suffer affliction with God's people instead of enjoying the passing pleasures of sin. The evidence of their faith was in their actions, not their feelings, and as they took action, God strengthened and matured their faith.

We see the same principle throughout the whole Bible. True faith is always linked to action. The woman with the issue of blood touched Jesus's garment (Matt. 9:20). The man with the withered hand reached out (12:13). The woman of Canaan wouldn't leave Jesus alone (15:21–28). Moses's mother put him in a basket (Ex. 2:3). Rahab hung a scarlet cord (Josh. 2:21). Esther went to see the king (Est. 4:15–5:2). None of these people knew for certain how their situations would turn out, but they took the first step. All of them must have had some feeling of fear or at least of uncertainty, but it wasn't that feeling that counted as faith; it was the action that showed their faith.

Our faith, too, must be linked to action. True saving faith is always accompanied by works (James 2:17). We do not have to have feelings of perfect confidence or lack fear in order to act on what God has commanded. We simply have to trust God enough to believe that He is good; that He offers truth in His word; and that we should think, speak, and act in accordance with it.

Hope Is More than Feeling or Desire

Hope is another example of something we tend to think of as a feeling, often about something that is uncertain. We "hope" that the weather will be nice, the lines will be short, and the traffic will be light on our way home. But the hope of the Bible involves so much more than how we would like our day to go or where we want life to take us. True hope involves a determined commitment (Heb. 10:23) to purposefully remind ourselves of truths (Lam. 3:21) that are absolutely certain (Titus 1:2) because they have been communicated to us by our God, who is utterly dependable (Ps. 33:18). Though we cannot yet physically see what we hope for (Rom. 8:24), we are still certain that it will come to pass, and our certainty allows us to both wait with patience (v. 25) and run with endurance (Heb. 12:1–2). And when we don't feel certain, then we know that we must make changes to what we are looking at, listening to, thinking, saying, and doing because the feeling that we label as hope involves each of these areas. It is possible by God's power to change what we place our hope in, and Scripture tells us how.

First, what we look at and listen to influences our hope. Each of us has unique interests, and we spend time learning about those interests through various forms of media. It is easy for us to get caught up in those interests and to begin placing our hope in them. We can tell what we are placing our hope in by how we feel when we don't get it. The person who bombards her eyes with pictures of beautiful décor from other people's homes may feel disappointed when her own home doesn't match up. The same goes for those who read productivity books when they don't finish their to-do list, those who watch fitness videos when they don't see the promised results in their bodies, and those who listen to business podcasts when their business isn't taking off. If we want to place less hope in these earthly things and more hope in eternal things, our first step is to give up some of the time we spend looking at and listening to all these social media accounts, books, videos, and podcasts in order to spend more time in the Bible. Ultimately, it is God who will change our hope, but He works through Scripture to do so, and so Scripture is what we must focus on.

Second, what we think influences what we place our hope in. First Peter 1:13 says, "Therefore gird up the loins of your mind, be sober, and rest your hope fully upon the grace that is to be brought to you at the revelation of Jesus Christ." To gird up the loins of our

minds is "to control what you think about, those things you decide
to set your mind upon."[13] Controlling our thoughts is something we
need to do in order to rest our hope on the grace of Jesus. Mark
Johnston observes, "When most people hear the word 'hope' they
instinctively think in terms of being optimistic that something might
happen. However, when Paul uses that term, he does so in the sense
of 'quiet certainty.' And the reason he can talk in terms of being sure
about what God has promised for the future is because of the fulfillment of all God had promised for the past."[14] Eugene Peterson
speaks of "making a map of the faithfulness of God, not charting the
rise and fall of our enthusiasms."[15] When we are feeling hopeless,
this is the pattern we should follow in our thinking. How has God
been faithful in the past, in our lives and in the lives of Christians
throughout history? If He has always been faithful in the past, can
we not trust Him to be faithful in the future? If we trust Him for the
future, how does that change our feelings and desires in the present?
Our thoughts should begin to sound more like those of so many of
the biblical authors talking themselves out of despair and into hope
in God by focusing on the future. In fact, we can use their exact
words by memorizing these verses and running them through our
minds over and over again when we feel despair:

> Why are you cast down, O my soul?
> And why are you disquieted within me?
> Hope in God, for I shall yet praise Him
> For the help of His countenance. (Ps. 42:5)

> This I recall to my mind,
> *Therefore* I have hope.

> Through the LORD's mercies we are not consumed,
> Because His compassions fail not.
> They are new every morning;

---

13. Guzik, Enduring Word Bible Commentary (website), on 1 Peter 1.
14. Mark G. Johnston, *Let's Study Colossians and Philemon* (Edinburgh: Banner
of Truth, 2013), 18.
15. Peterson, *Long Obedience in the Same Direction*, 133.

Great is Your faithfulness.
"The LORD is my portion," says my soul,
"Therefore I hope in Him!"

The LORD is good to those who wait for Him,
To the soul who seeks Him.
It is good that one should hope and wait quietly
For the salvation of the LORD. (Lam. 3:21–26)

There is laid up for me the crown of righteousness, which the
Lord, the righteous Judge, will give to me on that Day, and
not to me only but also to all who have loved His appearing.
(2 Tim. 4:8)

Third, what we hope in influences what we say and do, and what
we say and do influences where we place our hope. Because we know
eternity is coming, we should talk about what we're looking forward
to in heaven. Can you imagine how wonderful it will be to see Jesus
for the first time; to hear "Well done, My good and faithful servant";
to sing God's praises with so many other voices; to talk with the
Christians we have only ever read about in the Bible? We should also
be preparing for eternity by working to extend the kingdom of God.
Everything else should fade to the background and matter less in
light of eternity. What does it matter if we don't achieve every dream
we have for our earthly life? If we never live in the house we want
here, Jesus has prepared a place for us in heaven. If we never have
the type of relationships we want here, we will have sin-free relationships there. If we never quite fulfill the American dream, we will be
citizens not of America but of heaven. Let's speak and act like that is
true because it is true!

When what we look at, listen to, think, say, and do begins to
reflect the word of God more than the world, our hope stretches
from short-term to long-term. This is one of the marks of a Christian whose mind is set on things above. What happens tomorrow or
next week begins to matter less and less because our focus is more
and more on eternity. And what the world deems as success begins
to matter less because our focus is more on what God deems as faithfulness. A woman who is in labor does not set her hope in the end

of the next contraction but in the birth of her child, and a Christian who is still in this world does not set hope in the end of the next trial but in what these trials are leading to—being like Christ and being with Christ. John 16:21–22 says, "A woman, when she is in labor, has sorrow because her hour has come; but as soon as she has given birth to the child, she no longer remembers the anguish, for joy that a human being has been born into the world. Therefore you now have sorrow; but I will see you again and your heart will rejoice, and your joy no one will take from you." What we experience now is a light and momentary affliction compared to the glory that is coming (2 Cor. 4:17). Truths like this are what we should be looking at, listening to, thinking about, talking about, and acting on.

Love Is More than Feeling or Desire

We tend to think of love as merely a feeling, perhaps even more so than faith and hope. To think of love as a decision or a result of the choices we make feels entirely wrong to us. In part, this is because of the culture we live in. When our culture thinks of love, it thinks of an effortless, natural attraction to someone who makes us feel good. When the Bible speaks of love, though, it presents a completely different picture. The Bible speaks of love as obedience (1 John 5:3; 2 John 6), sacrifice (John 3:16; Eph. 5:2; 1 John 3:16), service (Gal. 5:13), labor (1 Thess. 1:3), forbearance (1 Cor. 13:4, 7; Eph. 4:2), effort (Matt. 22:37), and endurance (1 Cor. 13:7). The picture of love the Bible presents is less like a Hallmark movie and more like a man on His knees, sweating drops of blood, willing Himself to act against every fiber in His being in order to give up His life so that others might live (Luke 22:41–44). How can we follow His example?

First, what we look at and listen to influences how we think of love. If we are watching the content the world produces on the topic of love, then we will expect it to come easily. When it doesn't, we think that something is wrong. But if we are looking at the example of Christ and listening to the word of God, we will realize that love is not always an easy, natural feeling but that it requires effort.

Second, what we think of love influences how we act in love. One of the reasons we misunderstand what the Bible describes as love is that we have only one word—*love*—to describe what the original Greek of the New Testament has several different words for. When it refers to *agape*, the highest form of love, it is speaking of "a love more of decision than of the spontaneous heart; as much a matter of the mind than the heart, because it chooses to love the undeserving. 'Agape has to do with the mind; it is not simply an emotion which rises unbidden in our hearts; it is a principle by which we deliberately live' (Barclay)."[16] When we think of love in this way—not as merely feeling but as decision—we can decide to act in love even when we don't feel like doing the action that is required by love. This is what we see in the garden of Gethsemane. We do not see a man who desired to suffer. We see a man who wanted to love His people and therefore was willing to suffer. In order to follow Christ's example and love others, we don't have to desire to get up in the middle of the night to feed a crying baby, make a meal for a needy family, or respond with patience to a frustrated customer, but we do have to be willing to do these things because the decision to respond to others' needs is love.

Third, love influences what we say and do, and what we say and do influences how we love. Loving God is not only a sweeping feeling of adoration but includes obedience to His commands in all that we say and do. First John 5:3 states, "For this is the love of God, that we keep His commandments. And His commandments are not burdensome"; and in John 14:15 Jesus said, "If you love Me, keep My commandments." Elisabeth Elliot explains that the evidence of our love to God is obedience, not feelings. "We are given the choice, day by day, to choose good and refuse evil. Feelings will not, as a rule, help us very much. Although impulse is not invariably bad, more often than not the choice will be between principle and impulse. What I ought to do and what I feel like doing are seldom the same thing."[17]

---

16. Guzik, Enduring Word Bible Commentary (website), on Galatians 5.
17. Elliot, *Joyful Surrender*, 143.

We do not wait until we *feel* love for God in order to obey. We do not wait until we *desire* to show love to our neighbor in order to speak or act in love. This is what the world does. C. S. Lewis suggests, "Do not waste time bothering whether you 'love' your neighbor; act as if you did.... The worldly man treats certain people kindly because he 'likes' them: the Christian, trying to treat everyone kindly, finds himself liking more and more people as he goes on—including people he could not even have imagined himself liking at the beginning."[18] Because we are not yet perfectly sanctified, we know that our feelings are fickle and so we live and love out of obedience despite them. Tim and Kathy Keller write, "A loving person is not necessarily one who feels love for someone at the moment. Love is doing someone good, even if it means a sacrifice of your own interests. If you are filled with affection, there wouldn't be much sacrifice in it. Feelings tend to follow actions."[19] This is the beautiful reward of loving out of obedience— God transforms our feelings and desires so that we do begin more and more to feel love and to desire to show love.

The conclusion is this: follow your heart, but not always. Follow your heart when it lines up with Scripture. And when it doesn't, when what you feel and desire contradicts God and leads you toward disobedience, then follow God's word despite what your heart is telling you. Look to God and listen to His word not only when you feel like it but especially when you don't. Think on the things that God, not your flesh, wants you to think on. Let what you say and do be in obedience not to your heart but to God. And remember that though your feelings and desires can be deceitful above all things, God's word is truthful above all things, and He will use it to transform even the most desperately wicked heart that believes on the Lord Jesus Christ.

---

18. Lewis, *Mere Christianity*, 116–17.

19. Timothy Keller and Kathy Keller, *The Meaning of Marriage: A Couple's Devotional* (New York: Penguin Random House, 2019), July 9 entry.

—6—

THE MIND OF CHRIST

My extended family sat around the living room with mugs of coffee in hand and a sense of anticipation in the air. It was time to look at old photographs, to reminisce about the good old days, and to remember those who were no longer with us.

As the black-and-white pictures flashed across the screen, the questions started coming.

"Is that great-grandma?"

"I can't tell. It looks like her profile, but did she stand like that?"

Another picture. More questions.

"Mom, is that you when you were little? I can tell by the color of your hair!"

"Is that your brother behind you? He looked just like you."

Picture after picture, we used different physical features to figure out whose image we were looking at it. Though we were only looking at photographs, there were usually enough similarities between the person and the image for us to recognize him or her.

The same should be true of Christ and us. As Christians, we are being conformed to the image of Jesus Christ, and so there should be an ever-increasing number of similarities between us and Jesus, enough that others are able to recognize something of Him in us.

How is this possible? Though the people around us cannot know all that we look at, listen to, think, feel, or desire, they *can* know if we are speaking and acting in a Christlike way. The words they hear from our mouths and the actions they see us take can be a good indicator of what we are consuming, thinking, feeling, and desiring. We may be able to hypocritically fake all the right words and actions for a while, but those who know us well will be able to see over time whether we are becoming more or less Christlike.

We cannot become more like Him unless we behold Him (1 John 3:2), and the place to behold Him is in the Bible. Jesus is the only example we have of a human whose mind worked properly, according to the way God created our minds to work, and so we must study His life. What did Jesus look at and listen to? What did He think? What did He say and do? What did He feel and desire? How can we pull the answers to these questions down to the level of our everyday lives, allowing them to influence us at home, work, and church, changing how we interact with our family, friends, and neighbors? John Owen instructs,

> Look at his self-denial, his contempt of the world with its luxu-ries and comforts, his readiness for the cross, and his willingness to do or suffer according to the will of God. If this pattern is continually before us, it will effectively transform us more and more into his likeness. If we examine ourselves—the things we think about, the things that excite and interest us—and then compare our desires and thoughts with Christ's, we shall soon discover whether we possess his mind.[1]

The more we behold Christ, the more God renews our minds to be like the mind of Christ (1 Cor. 2:16; Phil. 2:5) and transforms our lives into His image (Rom. 12:2; 2 Cor. 3:18). This means we will begin looking, listening, and thinking the way He did; speaking and acting in ways that sound and look like Him; feeling and desiring the same things He felt and desired. This does not happen in our own strength, as if we could somehow copy Jesus and be magically changed. It happens by the power of the Spirit through what Jesus did for us in His life, death, and resurrection. He is not merely an example of how we should think and live but the way to a renewed mind, the truth that transforms us, and the resurrection life that

---

1. Owen, *Spiritual-Mindedness*, 218.

makes renewal and transformation possible in the first place. Let's study His mind and life to see what we can learn.

What Jesus Looked at and Listened To

From the beginning of what we know about Jesus's life, He was looking for wisdom from the words of His Father and listening to those who had wisdom. At just twelve years old, He was found by His parents in the temple, listening to the teachers, asking them questions, and astonishing everyone who heard Him (Luke 2:46–47). And what was the result of this listening and asking? He "increased in wisdom and stature, and in favor with God and men" (v. 52). What Jesus consumed from a very young age—the wisdom of His Father—helped to shape Him into who He would need to be.

When He was older, Jesus went into the wilderness and was tempted by the devil (Luke 4:1–13). Even though the temptations were strong, Jesus did not listen to or act on the devil's words. Instead, He responded with words that He had heard and learned from Scripture, from His Father. Those were the words He knew to be true, the words He had heard and memorized, the words that protected Him from the lies of Satan.

But Jesus did not depend only on verses He had memorized in the past. He knew that He needed an ongoing relationship with His Father, one that included regular times of speaking and listening. So He often went away from the crowds of people who were vying for His attention and healing to pray (Matt. 14:23; Mark 1:35; Luke 5:15–16; 9:28), sometimes even praying through the night (Luke 6:12). For Jesus, speaking to and hearing from His Father in prayer was not a bonus activity when He had extra time but a necessity that fueled the rest of His life and work. It was what He chose to do in the final hours before He was betrayed. It was what He needed to do in order to choose His Father's will over His own (Luke 22:39–44). And it was what He used His final breath to do (23:46).

If we are to live like Jesus, we too must look to God and listen to Him through Scripture and through prayer. It is not enough for us to decrease our consumption of all the various forms of media that the world puts out. We must fill that void with the wisdom of God by abiding in the word of God (John 15:7), allowing His words to have a stronger influence over us than our circumstances.[2]

This abiding will lead to renewing. Jesus is not just an example for us to follow but a living person for us to have a relationship with. Common sense tells us that over time we become more like the people we spend time with. If we are spending time with Jesus, we will become more like Him. We will be transformed by beholding Him (2 Cor. 3:17–18). By looking at and listening to Jesus by the power of the Holy Spirit, we will grow increasingly into His image.

What Jesus Thought

When Paul wrote to the Corinthians that "we have the mind of Christ" (1 Cor. 2:16) and instructed the Philippians to "let this mind be in you which was also in Christ Jesus" (Phil. 2:5), he was not just trying to be poetic. He really meant what he was saying. But how do we have the mind of Christ? Isn't this completely unattainable? What does this mean for us on a regular day in our lives?

In Philippians 2:5–11, Paul tells us to have the mindset of Christ and explains what that looks like in our lives.[3] In Jesus's mind, He did not think about what His own ambitions might be. He did not think of Himself as better than the people around Him. He did not think about only His own interests but the interests of those around Him. He thought about how He could obey God, and He acted on those thoughts. He could tell His disciples in Luke 22:27, "I am among you as the One who serves" because service and love to others was what His mind was centered on. Both in His thoughts and in the way He lived, Jesus perfectly fulfilled the Great Commandment to love God above all and our neighbor as ourselves (Mark 12:30–31).

If we know our own hearts, we recognize quickly that this is not a mindset we are able to just adopt in our own strength. It is

---

2. Ferguson, *Let's Study Philippians*, 102.
3. John Piper, "Have the Mind of Christ," Look at the Book, May 1, 2018, podcast, https://www.desiringgod.org/labs/have-the-mind-of-christ.

something that God works in His people over time as we walk by the Holy Spirit both in our actions and in our thought life. Elisabeth Elliot observes, "The word of Christ is, 'Love your enemies. Do good to them that hate you.' This is indeed impossible, as it was impossible for Peter to walk on the sea, until he obeyed the command. The mind made over from within begins to think Christ's thoughts after Him."[4]

Our minds begin to think Christ's thoughts after Him as we meditate on Him and His word, thinking about things that are true, honest, just, pure, lovely, of good report, and full of virtue and praise (see Phil. 4:8). Our mindset changes as we focus more on the things above and less on the things here below. The world is full of self-ish ambition and conceit, even seeing these things as virtues rather than vices. But we know better because we know from the mind of Christ that virtue is in humbling ourselves and counting others as better than we are and looking out for others' interests, not just our own. We know that our reward is in heaven and that the path we must take to get there requires us to take up our cross here. Elisabeth Elliot describes this mindset: "The Christlike mind counts for noth-ing what the world holds dear and holds as all-important what the world counts for nothing."[5]

Our thoughts begin to resemble Jesus's thoughts more and more as we bring them into captivity, comparing what pops into our minds with what is written in the Bible and preaching to ourselves if and when our thoughts do not line up with God's word. One way to do this is to hide God's word in our hearts so that we can use it like a sword to fight off Satan when He attacks us, as Christ did when He was tempted in the wilderness, a sword that is not just at home on our nightstands but in our minds and hearts, one that we can pull out and use at a moment's notice.

Our minds become more like His as we look back and forward. We look back by remembering God's past faithfulness to increase our faith, worship, witness, and hope. And we look forward in hope,

---

4. Elliot, *Joyful Surrender*, 62.
5. Elliot, *Joyful Surrender*, 74.

knowing by faith what we cannot see yet with our eyes, as Jesus did on the cross:

> Therefore we also, since we are surrounded by so great a cloud of witnesses, let us lay aside every weight, and the sin which so easily ensnares us, and let us run with endurance the race that is set before us, looking unto Jesus, the author and finisher of our faith, who for the joy that was set before Him endured the cross, despising the shame, and has sat down at the right hand of the throne of God.
>
> For consider Him who endured such hostility from sinners against Himself, lest you become weary and discouraged in your souls. (Heb. 12:1–3)

Jesus was able to endure the cross and to resist coming down from it (Matt. 27:40) even though He had legions of angels at His disposal (Matt. 26:53). How? By focusing on the joy set before Him. His hope for the future fueled His ability to stay on the cross in order to fulfill the Scriptures (v. 54) and save the people He loved. Let's follow His example and think His thoughts after Him. Let's consider Him and what He endured for us. This is the prescription given to us to fight off weariness and discouragement. Consider the joy that is set before you, the joy you will feel beyond your wildest imagination when you reach heaven's gates and see your Savior not just by faith but by sight. Consider that the joy set before Him included being surrounded by His people in heaven. Consider that if you believe in Him, you are part of that group of people. You are part of His joy. This was the mind of Christ. Let it be yours too.

What Jesus Said and Did

If we more and more have the mind of Christ, thinking His thoughts after Him, then it naturally follows that what we say and do should sound and look more and more like what He said and did. A prayer from *The Valley of Vision* reads, "May I . . . have the mind of Jesus, and tread in his steps."[6] This is the process of transformation. So what did He say and do in response to the circumstances of life? What do His responses show us about the way He thought? And how can we tread in His steps? Let's look at some examples.

One of the patterns that stands out when we read about Jesus's life throughout the Gospels is this: people asked Him for help, and He helped them. Even when He was traveling somewhere God had called Him to be, He helped those who asked (Mark 10:46–52). Even when He was on His way to help someone else, He helped whoever was in front of Him (Matt. 9:18–26). Even when He was trying to be alone, He helped those who followed Him (Luke 9:10–11). And when He helped, He addressed both the physical and spiritual needs of the person in front of Him.

What was the thought process that went on in Jesus's mind that led Him to help so many people, no matter the delay to His travel or the inconvenience to His life? Let's go back to the way Paul describes the mind of Christ in Philippians 2. Jesus esteemed others better than Himself and looked out for their interests and was willing even to take the form of a servant. He came not to be served but to serve (Mark 10:45). Because this was His mindset, it was only natural that He would choose to help those who needed His help. We are to do the same. After Jesus washed His disciples' feet, He said to them,

> Do you know what I have done to you? You call Me Teacher and Lord, and you say well, for so I am. If I then, your Lord and Teacher, have washed your feet, you also ought to wash one another's feet. For I have given you an example, that you should do as I have done to you. Most assuredly, I say to you, a servant is not greater than his master; nor is he who is sent greater than he who sent him. If you know these things, blessed are you if you do them. (John 13:12–17)

If we have the mind of Christ, considering others better than ourselves and remembering that servants are not greater than masters,

---

6. Arthur Bennett, ed., *The Valley of Vision: A Collection of Puritan Prayers and Devotions* (Edinburgh: Banner of Truth, 2014), 42.

then we too will help those whose needs we are aware of and able to meet, no matter the inconvenience to our lives. And the help we give to the least of those who are in Christ is help given to Christ Himself:

> Then the righteous will answer Him, saying, "Lord, when did we see You hungry and feed You, or thirsty and give You drink? When did we see You a stranger and take You in, or naked and clothe You? Or when did we see You sick, or in prison, and come to You?" And the King will answer and say to them, "Assuredly, I say to you, inasmuch as you did it to one of the least of these My brethren, you did it to Me." (Matt. 25:37–40)

Another pattern that we see in Jesus's life was that when faced with a choice between His own will and His Father's, He chose His Father's. This was His food (John 4:34). This was the reason He came down from heaven (6:38). This was His pattern from childhood until death. When His parents found Him in the temple at twelve years old, Jesus asked them, "Why did you seek Me? Did you not know that I must be about My Father's business?" (Luke 2:49). When He was in the garden of Gethsemane before His death on the cross, He prayed, "Father, if it is Your will, take this cup away from Me; nevertheless not My will, but Yours, be done" (Luke 22:42). And between these events, we see countless examples of the same willingness to do His Father's will despite what His own will was. Elisabeth Elliot writes, "There was a tremendous battle being waged between His natural human response to what was happening and His absolute desire to do the will of the Father. He had come to earth expressly to do that will. His purpose was simple. Carrying it out, however, was not easy. He could not possibly 'feel comfortable' with it. But He did it. That is what matters. He did it."[7]

What went on in Jesus's mind that allowed Him to do His Father's will when it was different from His own? Again, we find the answer in Philippians 2. Paul tells of how Jesus "humbled Himself and became obedient to the point of death, even the death of the cross" (v. 8). Even though He was God, He was willing to take the

---

7. Elliot, *Joyful Surrender*, 142.

form of a servant and obey to the point of death because He had a mindset of humility. He knew that He would be exalted in the future in heaven (vv. 9–11), and He did not need additional exaltation here on earth. We too will be exalted one day if we humble ourselves now (1 Peter 5:6), so we don't need to worry about being exalted now. If our mindset is humble like Christ's, we too will be willing to follow God's will even when it contradicts our own, saying with John the Baptist, "He must increase, but I must decrease" (John 3:30).

The way Jesus helped other people and the way He obeyed are just two examples of how His thinking influenced His words and actions, but there are countless more. In our lives too, words and actions come as a result of how we think and influence how we think. So we must be careful to think about the things that will make us more like Christ: who God is; who we are in Christ; what God's will is for us; how God makes us like Jesus; the effort, learning, and strategy required for obedience; the reward of obedience; and how suffering leads to glory. If we are imitating Christ's way of thinking, it is only natural that we will begin to imitate His way of talking and walking: "Therefore be imitators of God as dear children. And walk in love, as Christ also has loved us and given Himself for us, an offering and a sacrifice to God for a sweet-smelling aroma" (Eph. 5:1–2).

What Jesus Felt and Desired

Part of what happens when God conforms us to the image of Christ is that He conforms our feelings and desires to what Christ felt and desired. Jesus had normal (though not sinful) human feelings and desires. He felt sadness and anger in addition to hope and joy. He desired food and friendship. But the difference between Him and us is that He did not follow His feelings and desires to the point of sin. When He had to choose between His Father's will and giving in to a normal human desire, He always denied Himself and chose His Father's will. This was because His desire to do His Father's will was greater than His desire to do His own will. This was how He habitually lived, and we too should be habitually living in such a way that God's will always wins out in our lives. This is a work of the

Holy Spirit. Without His power, we are powerless to change our own feelings and desires. Yet He works through the circumstances and decisions of our lives, including what we look at and listen to, what we think, and what we say and do. Transformation happens in conjunction with all these other choices. And as it happens, what we feel and desire begins to look less like the natural sinful human response and more like the responses of Jesus. Let's look at some examples of how Jesus responded to various situations to get an idea of what this should look like in our lives.

First, Jesus chose faith over fear. When He was with His disciples in a boat on the Sea of Galilee and a storm came up, Jesus remained calm and even slept in the storm (Mark 4:37–41). How was this possible? Jesus was human as well as divine. How could He have so little fear and such great faith? It was possible because His entire life had been a practice of trusting His Father. He knew His Father so well that He couldn't help but trust Him. He had looked to His Father in every difficult situation throughout His life and had always received help. His thoughts about His Father were not thoughts of doubt but thoughts of love and trust. And He always spoke and acted according to that love and trust. He had always lived out of faith, and a storm did not change how He lived.

He tells us to do the same. When the future looks dark and impossible and we feel only fear, when we don't seem to have even a mustard seed of faith, Jesus tells us what to look at, what to think, and what to say to fight fear. He tells us to *look* at the birds (Matt. 6:26). Have you done this? Have you really gone outside and looked at the birds, letting every bird you see be a flying reminder of the fact that God cares for them, that you are of more value than they, and that you can logically conclude that He will care for you too? Jesus tells us to *think* about the lilies of the field (v. 28). Have you done this? Have you thought about flowers and how beautiful they are, even though they have no ability to think about what they look like? Do you let every flower you see remind you that you do not need to worry about what you will eat, drink, or wear? Jesus tells us not to *say* our anxious questions but to seek first the kingdom of God. Have you done this? Have you turned your thoughts and your life from dwelling on the what ifs to focusing on the sure kingdom of God? Have you traded in your anxious questions for trusting questions?

> The LORD is on my side;
> I will not fear.
> What can man do to me?
> (Ps. 118:6)

This was how Jesus lived. This was how He could have faith and not fear. This is how you can too.

Second, Jesus chose hope over despair. The Bible tells us that this was how He was able to endure the cross, despise the shame of His death, and endure so much hostility—because of the joy that was set before Him (Heb. 12:2). How could this be? How could there be enough joy in this world to get Him through that amount of suffering? Again, our answer can be found in how He lived His entire life. He placed more value on what His Father said than on the words of Satan or other people. His mind was set not on temporary things here below, like comfort or fulfillment, but on eternal things above, and what He said and did reflected that. He lived as if eternity and heaven were real and of more value than time and earth—because they are. He was able to empty Himself here (Phil. 2:7) because God would exalt Him there (vv. 9–11).

The author of Hebrews tells us how we can live in this way too by explaining what to look at, what to think, and what to do. He tells us to *look* to Jesus in order to lay aside sin and run the race with endurance (12:1–2). Do you do this? Do you see that Jesus is the author and finisher of your faith? Do you see the way He endured and the way He was rewarded for that endurance? Does His reward remind you of your future reward and encourage you to endure? The author of Hebrews also tells us to *think* about how Jesus endured so that we can fight weariness and discouragement in our souls (v. 3). Do you do this? When you are feeling weary and discouraged, do you take control of your mind and intentionally think about how Jesus must have felt in the garden, sweating drops of blood? Returning to His disciples only to find them sleeping during His desperate hour of need? Looking at Peter, one of His closest earthly friends, after he had denied Him three times? Do you think about how discouraging that must have been? How weary Jesus must have been when He was carrying His cross after being up all night, scourged and tormented for sin that was not His own? Surely these thoughts can encourage us to keep going in our Christian walk. The author of Hebrews also tells us what to *do*—to endure chastening because of the fruit of righteousness produced in those who are trained by it (vv. 7–11). Are you doing this? If you are looking to Jesus and considering how He endured, can you also endure? Can you focus on these beautiful words—"nevertheless, afterward"—even though we have not reached that blessed "afterward" yet? This is what hope is—not a mere feeling that pops up here and there but a certainty of what is to come that motivates a Christlike way of living and enduring now.

Third, Jesus chose love over hate. How was this possible when so many of the people around Him hated Him? It was possible because of His mindset. He knew that His Father loved Him, and so He was able to love other people (John 15:9). When He thought of other people, He counted them as more significant than Himself, despite the fact that He is God (Phil. 2:3–7). Because He saw others as more significant, He looked and listened less to the interests of His own flesh and more to theirs (v. 4). And because His focus was on the interests of others, what He said and did throughout His life was servant-like and obedient, to the point of death (vv. 7–8). This is love—not merely a life-giving feeling but a mindset and lifelong series of decisions in which we give up our lives for others (John 15:13).

How can we do this when it goes against every fiber of our sinful human natures? John explains how in his first epistle by telling us where to look, who to listen to, and what to say and do. He tells us to *look* at what kind of love the Father has given (1 John 3:1) and to *listen* to those who are from God (4:6). When we do this, we will see that Jesus laid down His life for us and that what we should *do* in response is to lay down our lives for others (3:16; 4:11). After all, love is not just in what we *say* but in what we *do* (3:18), and it is only possible because God first loved us (4:19). The scribe in Mark 12 sums it up well when he tells Jesus, "Well said, Teacher. You have spoken the truth, for there is one God, and there is no other but He. And to love Him with all the heart, with all the understanding, with all the soul, and with all the strength, and to love one's neighbor as oneself, is more than all the whole burnt offerings and sacrifices" (vv. 32–33). Jesus's response to the scribe was, "You are not far from the kingdom of God" (v. 34). Love will take every ounce of effort and energy that we have, but the reward is great—to know Christ, to be like Him, and to be part of His kingdom. How could we desire anything else?

AFTERWORD

> The first of all the commandments is: "Hear, O Israel, the LORD our God, the LORD is one. And you shall love the LORD your God with all your heart, with all your soul, with all your mind, and with all your strength." This is the first commandment. And the second, like it, is this: "You shall love your neighbor as yourself." There is no other commandment greater than these. (Mark 12:29–31)

This was Jesus's answer when He was asked which commandment is the first of all, and it covers everything. There is no part of our bodies, minds, souls, or lives that is exempt from loving the Lord and our neighbor. And there is no part that is disconnected from the other parts. What we see with our eyes and hear with our ears has great influence over our thoughts, and so we must be consuming the word of God far more than the wisdom of the world. Our thoughts physically change our brains, renew our minds, and motivate what we say and do, and so we must be thinking according to the word of God. Everything we say and do changes our thoughts, feelings, and desires. And what we feel and desire is always more than mere feeling and desire, changing how we think and how we live.

This is not a negative thing. This is how we were created, and it is good! Every part of our lives is meant to work in connection with every other part. And when each part is working correctly—in obedience to God and His word—then the result is love for God and love for our neighbor. We see this in Jesus's life. Everything He looked at, listened to, thought, said, did, felt, and desired was out of obedience to His Father, and the result was a love so strong it took Him to the cross. He died so that we might live. He gave us His Spirit so that we might set our minds on the things of the Spirit and live according to the Spirit. He renews us so that we might be transformed, for our good and His glory.

> As for me, I will see Your face in righteousness;
> I shall be satisfied when I awake in Your likeness.
> (Ps. 17:15)